Copyright August 2014 by Ian Watts

All rights reserved. No part of this publication may be reproduced, distributed, or transmitted in any form or by any means, including photocopying, recording, or other electronic or mechanical methods, without the prior written permission of the publisher, except in the case of brief quotations embodied in critical reviews and certain other non-commercial uses permitted by copyright law. For permission requests, write to the publisher, addressed "Attention: Permissions Coordinator," at the address below.

Ian Watts and Tim Trafford assert their moral rights to be identified as the author of this book.

LPL Publications
10 Anderson Road
Salisbury
Wiltshire
SP1 3DX
United Kingdom

Table of Contents

Chapter	Subject	Page
1	Physical Security	4
	Identifying the Problem and Finding Solutions	5
	Risk Assessments	9
	Developing Solutions	10
	Cost/Benefit Analysis	16
	Which Supplier to choose?	24
2	Access Control	30
	Manual Access Control	31
	Electronic Access Control	37
	ID Cards	51
	Biometrics	55
3	Closed Circuit Television (CCTV)	73
	Types Of System	78
	CCTV Surveys	84
	CCTV Evidence	96
	Protection of Data	101
	Data Protection Act 1998, (DPA 1998)	102

Chapter	Subject	Page
4	Alarm Systems	122
	Intruder Alarms	122
	Alarm Panels	128
	Alarm Surveys	135
	Product Protection	144
5	Personnel	156
	In-House Security Teams	157
	Non-Dedicated security teams	165
	Third party security specialists	168
	Conclusion	182
	About the authors	183

Chapter 1

Physical Security

Introduction

In this book we will examine the approaches that can be considered when deciding which physical security measures should be implemented within a retail business. As will be seen from some of the methods that will be discussed, it does not necessarily follow that the more 'hi tech' or expensive the methods adopted are, the greater effect they will have. Sometimes the most effective and cost efficient methods implemented can be the most basic and simple methods available.

To begin this book we are going to look at some general issues relating to the loss prevention specialist's work. Within this book there are several references to legislation. As the book has been written primarily for loss prevention specialists working in the United Kingdom, the legislation quoted tends to be UK legislation. Nonetheless, almost every jurisdiction now has similar legislation and it is the responsibility of any loss prevention specialist to familiarise themselves with it. Where such legislation does not exist in a particular jurisdiction, the details found in this book will assist a loss prevention department in formulating their organisation's procedural rules and codes of conduct

It must also be taken into consideration that, in the case of larger businesses especially, many organisations operate internationally. It is not sufficient, therefore, for a loss prevention specialist to know the laws and regulations of their own jurisdictions, they must also have a working knowledge of the laws and regulations in other jurisdictions in which they may have to operate. Crime is now a global phenomenon and criminals take no notice of international boundaries unless it is for their benefit. For example, crimes committed in the USA could involve criminals operating in the UK and laws in both countries will apply to any investigation being conducted.

Identifying the Problem and Finding Solutions

The difference between an effective loss prevention and risk  management department and an ineffective one, is that a good one is always proactive in identifying both existing and potential problems. As the majority of Company Boards of Directors will confirm, no matter how successful a business is in terms of the profits that it is making, there is always room for improvement. The reason for this is because no matter how large the loss prevention and risk management department is within the business, or how much money is spent on protecting the businesses assets, there will always be events taking place that will be the cause of ongoing known and unknown shrinkage.

Recognising the Issues

The first thing that needs to be done before committing resources of any kind to a problem, whether these resources are of the financial, manpower or technological kind, is to be able to recognise what the challenges are. There is a very simple way of achieving this knowledge and that is by first fully understanding the business.

Unfortunately many loss prevention and risk management professionals go wrong by assuming that the knowledge they have obtained while working for other businesses will work in their current organisation. This is rarely the case because different organisations have different strategies, different resources to apply to loss prevention and different attitudes to loss prevention. This 'one size fits all' attitude could not be further from the truth. Every business is different, even ones that operate in similar sectors.

An example of this situation is that despite the fact that Asda, Tesco's, Sainsbury's and WM Morrison's are all major supermarket chains who, in the main, provide a similar of retail service to their customers, they nevertheless each have their own loss prevention and risk management issues. Each Company will deal with the issues in accordance with their individual Company's values and in some cases traditional or preferred operating practices.

Learning the Company

There are many ways of getting to know the business that you will be expected to protect:

Induction - One method that is almost always implemented is through a Company induction process. Inductions can range from being very brief, general affairs, designed for all new employees, to more complex, specifically formulated inductions, designed to inform individuals of all aspects of the areas of business that they are likely to encounter or be involved with. The purpose of the 'general' induction is mainly to explain initial administration topics such as pay, general employment terms and conditions, and to provide a brief outline of Company procedures. The more in-depth induction will involve presentations from different departments to explain the functions and expectations of the departments in relation to employee's actions. It is always helpful if the loss prevention department can make a presentation to new staff as honest staff are the best asset protection you can find.

Personal Research – You will no doubt have conducted research into the Company or organisation before going for a job interview and this should have given you important information about financial matters and Company values. Do it again once you have been offered a position – in depth! Check the organisation's trading figures, get a copy of the financial accounts and research the key personnel. In short, find out whatever you can about the workings of the organisation and who makes it work. All information is useful.

Working Relationships - Irrespective of the management level that loss prevention and risk management operatives will be expected to work at, a good working relationship should be established with corresponding management levels in all areas of the business. To achieve this the loss prevention specialist should make a point of visiting every department and spending time with the staff employed in them to understand their roles and objectives. This will also help you to better understand the overall objectives of the business. Regional, Area and departmental meetings are always a fantastic opportunity to learn what is going on and to network.

Work in Other departments - If there is an opportunity to spend some time working in other departments of the business it should be seized with both hands. Not only will you gain excellent knowledge of procedures, you will learn what the staff like and don't like (don't like often means cutting corners or ignoring a policy altogether) and, most importantly, you will learn about the different personalities employed within the departments. Until you have a clear understanding of how the business operates, the Directors' objectives and aims for the business and the policies and procedures used within the business, it is almost impossible to create an effective loss prevention and risk management strategy that is compatible with the business aims and objectives.

Risk Assessments

In profit protection, assessing risk is the process of determining the level of risk that could be associated with a particular situation or course of action. This is very different to the risk assessments conducted in respect of Health and Safety for example. There you are only concentrating on hazards and risks which will or could affect the health, safety and welfare of staff, contractors and visitors. In dealing with the identified risks, profit is often drained from a business as measures are put in place to minimise the risks. Profit protection, as the name implies, is looking at the risks associated with the loss of revenue or assets from a business by whatever cause, which would include money spent on H & S initiatives. Sometimes there is a degree of conflict between the two.

Why Conduct Risk Assessments?

Conducted properly, irrespective of the subject matter, risk assessments are an essential providing direction at all levels of responsibility. This makes them an ideal tool for the profit protection and risk management practitioners. It is important to realise though that risk assessments should be tailor made for the department of the business to be evaluated. It is most definitely not a case of 'one size fits all'.

In some cases the challenges that need to be addressed will be blatantly obvious but in other situations it will not be so easy to identify them. Regardless of which category they fall into, the starting point for dealing with them will be the risk assessment. Once this has been completed a careful and detailed analysis of the findings should be carried out. This will identify the issues to be addressed. From this point it is necessary to develop solutions which deal with the issues.

Developing Solutions

The challenges involved in developing effective solutions to business issues are really twofold: they don't often come from a text book and they invariably cost money or other resources. The loss prevention specialist's primary concern is the cost effective use of resources in order to maximise profits for 'their' organisation. For this reason it is a poor loss prevention specialist who does not take resources into consideration when proposing solutions. The s of resources normally found in an organisation will include:

Finance – the obvious and generally first thought of resource. It is no good proposing a system costing tens of thousands of pounds to an organisation that is currently losing money unless the expense will result in that loss being turned into profit.

Personnel – are the personnel available to implement the solutions in relation to numbers and expertise. If the solution requires the recruitment of a specialist on a salary of £50k a year, the result needs to be a saving considerably in excess of that.

Time – normally relating to personnel, do the proposals take into consideration the amount of time that people will have to spend meeting them. For example, a staff search policy could reduce staff theft considerably but while the security officers are conducting staff searches, who is watching the shop floor? Will the organisation spend money to increase security officer numbers so that the shop floor is not left unprotected

Physical Assets – what this chapter is all about and will include mechanical, electronic and human resources – all of which can be very expensive.

This is not an exhaustive list. The full list of resources will change from organisation to organisation.

Generally, solutions can be divided into the following categories:

> (a) **Quick-fix solutions** – Little financial costs to the business – This could be something as simple as making sure that security procedures that are already in place are followed.

(b) **Quick-fix solutions** – Minor financial costs to the business - This could be the preparation and distribution of a loss prevention manual to all branches within a retail business

(c) **Medium to long term solutions** - (6 – 12 months) - Small financial cost to the business. This could be visiting all of the retail branches to ensure that loss prevention procedures are being implemented.

(d) **Medium to long term solutions** - (6 -12 months) - Minor financial costs to the business. This could be holding security training courses in each of the retail Regions.

(e) **Long term solutions** (12 months or more) – Major financial costs to the business – This could be a plan to upgrade all of the CCTV systems in the retail branches to ones that have a digital function.

The loss prevention and risk management strategy that will be produced for consideration by the business as a result of analysing the risk assessments will probably produce a mix of solutions. It should be stressed that it is not the role, nor is it normally within the expertise of the loss prevention specialist, to produce a definitive strategy for a business. To attempt to do so would suggest that the loss prevention specialist has detailed knowledge of all aspects of the business plan, management strategies across all departments and available resources. That would never be the case.

5 questions have to be answered by the proposed solutions:

1. What are the risks to the organisation's bottom line by doing nothing?

2. What resources are available to deal with the risks or problem?

3. What viable solutions are available *(all options should be fully researched, costed and presented. It is not the loss prevention specialist's role to decide which option to implement)*

4. What are the benefits to the organisation if proposed solutions are implemented?

5. What are the costs to the business of implementing the proposed solutions?

One of the main things a loss prevention specialist should remember is that they are not the owners of the business or organisation. Many times the loss prevention personnel will make proposals that will be dismissed by senior managers. DO NOT TAKE IT PERSONALLY ! There could be many reasons for this but never let it be because you have not done your job properly. You conduct comprehensive research and present the facts but others will make the decisions about use of resources, expenditure and projects.

Choosing Appropriate Methods (Proportionality)

There are numerous methods which could be implemented for protecting the assets of a business. The trick for loss prevention specialists is to identify the methods which provide a proportionate response to the threat or perceived risk. Doing so will mean the adopted solutions are more likely to be useful and cost effective.

An example of this approach would be where low-value confectionary items are being stolen from a retail outlet. The first approach would be to try and identify when the items were being taken. It may be that the thefts are occurring during school lunch times and just after schools close for the day. If this was the case then the first course of action could be to ensure that there is a staff member or security guard present in or around the vulnerable areas of the shop at the appropriate times. It would not be to immediately install a fifteen camera, face recognition digital CCTV system, monitored by a 'Third Party' Company, costing thousands of pounds.

Practicalities

Although available resources have a major impact on deciding which solutions could be adopted, they are not the only consideration. Thought must also be given to:

14

- The business plan, aims and objectives
- Store layout and practicalities of changing it
- Size of the retail outlet
- Access points for customers and staff
- Measures already in place
- Policies, procedures and working practices
- Technological expertise of staff who may be required to use new equipment
- Management issues such as recruitment and change management
- HR issues such as trade union agreements and consultation with staff representatives
- Productivity issues if staff are asked to change the way they work or have to do more tasks to fulfil their role. Electronic tagging can be very effective in preventing or deterring theft but it also adds time *(albeit very little)* to customer transactions. This may lead to longer queuing time for customers during busy periods.

All of these can affect decisions about the solutions to be considered. Let's look at store layout as an example.

High value perfumes are being stolen in large quantities from a chain of retail stores. It may be a practical solution to recommend that the perfumes should only be displayed near to the point of sale, where they can be monitored by the staff, thus deterring would-be shoplifters. In a similar example, however, if a large supermarket is having problems with significant quantities of wines and spirits being stolen by shoplifters, it would not be a practical solution to try and move these product items nearer too, or behind the point of sale. Firstly the point of sale area would not be large enough to accommodate them, and even if they could be displayed behind the sales counter, this would be defeating the object of the business, which is the process of allowing the genuine customers direct access to the products before purchasing them.

Cost/Benefit Analysis

Once an appropriate method has been identified that is believed to be suitable for dealing with the problem, it usually follows that approval will be required for the implementation of that method. In most businesses the approval will be required at management levels, such as the Head of a department or Operations, and or the Financial Director. For larger projects requiring major financial investment; it may require the approval of the Board of Directors. Irrespective of the level at which approval is required, the application for expenditure must always be accompanied by a detailed cost benefit analysis. The main purpose of a cost benefit analysis is to establish:

- The projected benefits of implementing the recommendations.

- Evidence as to whether the financial expenditure will be either more or less than the expected benefits.

- The projected Return On Investment (ROI), especially if the initial costs outweigh the perceived short term benefits.

Apart from the potential financial ramifications of getting it wrong, getting into the habit of conducting a cost benefit analysis prior to submitting a recommendation for approval, can in the long run save a lot of time and embarrassment. The benefits of conducting a cost benefit analysis to the person submitting any proposal will include:

- Improved research skills

- Ability to answer detailed financial questions about the proposal

- The ability to abandon the proposal if the figures do not 'add up'.

- A better understanding of how business works

It should of course be remembered that no matter how good the recommendations for a new project may look on paper, it still does not mean that they will automatically be approved by those holding the purse strings. This could be for a number of reasons. The application for approval was made at the end of a financial year and there is no funding available for it, or those responsible for approving the recommendations are aware of additional influential factors that have not been accounted for during the compilation of the cost benefit analysis. It may therefore be the case that the recommendations will have to be re- submitted at a more appropriate time and possibly after they have been modified to account for the previously unknown factors.

If, on modification, the benefits of the recommendations are not too dissimilar to the original costs, or are less than the original costs, those responsible for the approval have a choice of three options:

1. Request that the recommendations be modified in some way that would either reduce the costs and/or enhance the benefits

2. Reject the recommendations

3. Approve the recommendations regardless of cost

The latter option is the least likely of the three options, unless there is a view that the benefits could be realised as part of a long term project.

If the recommendations for financial expenditure are approved, then there will be expectations from those that authorised the expenditure that the expected benefits will be realised.

Provided that the projected benefits that were submitted were not exaggerated during the process of compiling the cost benefit analysis, then this should not be a problem and the whole process will not have been a waste of time or money.

In order to stand a fairly good chance of being successful with a recommendation for expenditure, consideration of the following points may help:-

- **Timing** - A good Manager always thinks ahead, so try and put forward proposals that will coincide with forthcoming budget proposals. There is no point asking for money if the pot is likely to be empty at the time proposals are submitted for consideration.

- **Realistic Cost Benefit Analysis** – Do not exaggerate the benefits of the recommendations. If anything slightly understate them, then there will be no disappointments. Always try to deliver more than you promise.

- **Research** – Make sure that where requests for expenditure relating to technological items of equipment are being made that:-

    o The capabilities of the equipment have been fully researched

    o That both the short term and long term life expectancy of the equipment has been assessed

- o That the best possible price has provisionally been negotiated with the supplier
- **Flexibility** – When submitting a cost benefit analysis for approval, if possible include more than one option for consideration. The options can be along the lines of; what would be the ideal solution, what could also work and what at the very least would do.
- **Reputation** – Develop a reputation based on the fact that previous requests for expenditure have always met expectations and ultimately have 'produced the goods'.

New Technology

When you think there is nothing else left in this world to be invented or improved upon, something new always hits the market. This is particularly the case for equipment used in the loss prevention and risk management industry.

It is mind blowing to look at some of the innovations that have come about in the last ten years alone. Things that we now take for granted and expect as a matter of course. Telephones are not just used for making calls but have to be truly mobile. They must have the capability to take photographs, record video footage and access the internet. In fact, smartphones have become a serious threat to loss prevention due to their data handling capabilities.

The retail industry invests millions of pounds every year, not only in order to operate in a cost effective and efficient manner, but also in an attempt to protect its most important assets; its people, real estate, data and stock. Unfortunately it does not follow that the more money that is invested in protecting people, real estate, data and stock, the safer they will be. In recent years detailed and protracted intellectual studies into the effectiveness of basic CCTV systems would suggest that CCTV adds little or no value at all in deterring either theft or assaults. It is therefore important that before consideration is given for initial or further investment in technology, whether it be new, or established, that it will satisfy the demands and expectations of the business and will provide returns commensurate to the money spent on it.

The use of new technology can be the cause of numerous problems, such as:-

- Technology is generally more expensive when it first becomes available for general purchase.

- There are quite often teething problems in relation to the actual performance of new technology.

- It can be quite expensive and difficult to maintain as spare parts may not be generally available. There will also be limited numbers of engineers trained to maintain and repair new technology.

- New technology may not be compatible with technologies already being used within the business. This is especially true where computer software is involved.

- In extreme cases the technology may not prove popular and therefore be discontinued or superseded.

Keeping Up To Date

At times it can be quite daunting trying to keep pace with the changes in technology. The best way to keep up to date and current with the changes is by subscribing to the trade magazines and publications. In addition to trade magazines and other publications there are a number of trade shows that take place each year, where products of all s are on show and being demonstrated. The biggest annual trade show event in the UK, is the International Fire and Security Exhibition and Conference (IFSEC) that usually takes place each May at the NEC Birmingham.

Trials

When considering the implementation of new technology, research is the key to avoiding disappointment. Make enquires with organisations who already use the technology. Contact them either by telephone, internet or better still a personal visit, so that you can see the product in action and also get the user's views on the product. Ask plenty of questions such as, is it doing what it is supposed to do? Have there been any problems with it? Were the problems easily resolved? What is the after sales service like with the Company it was purchased from? The true answers to this research cannot be found in the contents of a glossy sales brochure, but will be invaluable in helping to decide if the product will be suitable for your proposed security strategy.

One potential pitfall to be aware of regarding brand new technology, particularly if the business that you are working for is a large one that the general public are familiar with, is that some suppliers and manufactures will try and sell you new technology that is neither tried nor tested. Their purpose is to allow them to advertise the product, 'as used by ABC Company' as an attempted giving the product credibility. Their offer may be very tempting but do not fall for it.

Choosing a Supplier

Having conducted all of the relevant risk assessments and decided on the of security measures that will best suit the needs of the business, a decision will then need to be made as to which Company to use in order to get the job done. Most large Companies operate with a list of 'Approved Suppliers'. These are usually Companies that your business already has contracts with or has used in the past. If this is the situation it is still good practice to follow the guidelines that we will shortly be going through. Circumstances often change, as do standards and costs!

With so many different Companies providing similar services and only too happy to take your money, it can be a minefield when it comes to selecting the right one. You need suppliers that will provide value for money, goods or services that meet the expected standards and that are not going to let you, and ultimately the business, down. In order to try and get it right we will now look at the points that should be taken into consideration before allowing any works to go ahead or services to be provided.

Which Supplier to choose?

The old saying 'horses for courses' best sums up the answer to this question. Do not use the first person that claims that they can do the job. Shop around and only look at companies that specialise in what you will be asking them to do or provide. It is better to keep away from companies that claim that they can do everything. The reason being, well having started this paragraph with an old saying we may as well finish with one, 'Jack of all trades, Master of none'.

Firstly put together a short list of companies that have been researched from sources, or that have been recommended by people that used them before. Also maybe include one or two companies that are on the business's 'Approved Suppliers' list. Make sure you can positively answer the following questions:

1. Do they specialise in what you are going to be asking them to do or supply?

2. Do they have the required qualifications and accreditations to do the work?

3. Can they work with the specific s of equipment that you want installed?

4. Have they undergone the appropriate training to install the equipment that you want?

5. Is the Company big enough to be able to handle the volume of work that you are going to expect them to do?

6. What are their prices like?

7. Are the prices negotiable?

8. Are they a local or national Company?

9. Can they provide references from businesses that they are now working with, or already have worked with?

10. Are they listed at companies House and do they appear to be a financially sound company to do business with?

25

11. Do they Sub contract?

Once a list of several companies has been put together a tendering process can begin.

The Tendering Process

In order to get the best out of the tendering process it is recommended that a minimum of three but no more than five companies should be selected from the list and invited to tender for the work. In order to be fair to the companies that are expected to tender, they should all be asked the same questions, with no clues given as to what the required answers should be. The questions asked will be basically the same as the ones already covered above but would also include additional questions such as:-

1. Do they give discounts for large orders, or certain sized contracts?
2. How long will it take them to do the job or provide the service?
3. When could they do the job or provide the service?
4. What liability cover do they have?
5. What after sales services do they provide?
6. Will they agree to work to your business' Terms and Conditions?

7. The notice periods for both parties to terminate a contract should one be awarded

8. Their payment conditions, 30 days, three months etc.

9. Will they give an additional discount for prompt payments?

10. How do they invoice? i.e.. one job one invoice or collectively, i.e. a summary of invoices with the individual invoices attached.

(NB) Remember to provide details of the deadline for the tendering process. Tenders received after the deadline date should be disregarded.

Once all of the companies that have been asked to tender have returned their applications then the information that they have supplied should be carefully studied. If any of the answers that they have supplied are ambiguous in any way they should be clarified before the Company in question is considered further. Any ambiguities that cannot be resolved, then the Company in question should be removed from the tendering process.

Contracts

Having decided which Company to use and provisionally agreed a price, the process should not progress any further until contracts have been signed by both parties. Contracts should detail the agreed expectations of both parties. Before any form of contract is signed off it will need to have been fully checked, by either a specialist within the business, such as someone that has this kind of responsibility in the Estates department, or, if appropriate, the solicitors that normally represent the business. Finally it will then have to be approved by the budget holder as being in accordance with the original request for expenditure.

Budgets

Once the work is under way or the services are being provided careful management of the project is necessary to ensure that agreed budgets are not exceeded. This should be an ongoing process from the time the contract starts, as it will be easier to deal with any problems as they arise rather than trying to sort everything out later on down the line.

One word of warning - most companies work on the basis of an annual incremental rise of costs and this is usually applied to the charges in the form of a percentage figure. It can range from 1% to 3% in some cases, so this will need to be discussed and planned for within the financial budget.

Key Performance Indicators (KPIs)

KPIs are used in ways within a business. They are often used during appraisal processes with employees to set performance targets for the employee. In this context, however, they are used to set out performance targets between a business and a contractor. Evidence that the contractor is meeting any contractually agreed KPIs should be obtained within the agreed time parameters. If there are any problems with KPIs then they should be addressed with the contractor at the earliest opportunity in order that they can rectify the situation. If they fail to do so and/or continue to fall short of the agreed KPIs, then the termination of their contract and possible legal action should be considered.

Chapter 2

Access Control

Access control can be split into two categories; manual access control and electronic access control. Although the term access control sounds like a modern one, access control in its manual form has been around since cavemen started placing wooden fences across the front of their caves to help stave off attacks from neighbouring warring tribes. Today, a mortice lock on your front door is non-other than a form of access control.

The general term access control can equally be applied to passwords on a computer or chip and PIN to access bank accounts at an ATM. For the specific purpose of loss prevention and risk management we are referring to the controlled access of premises or certain areas within premises, by either manual or electronic means. Access control is generally viewed as the second tier in the security of a physical structure.

Even in its most basic form access control is of prime importance when seeking to secure premises or protect the people and business assets within. It should therefore follow that the more important it is that things are to be protected, the greater the level of access control there should be. We will now examine a selection of some of the s of manual and electronic access control methods that are presently available and highlight some of the advantages and disadvantages that they have to offer the loss prevention and risk management industry.

Manual Access Control

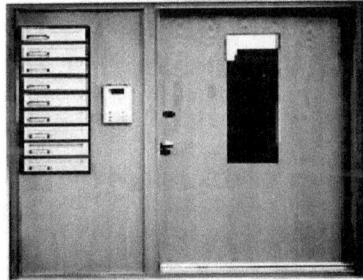

For the purpose of this section the term manual access control means the control of access by means that do not involve electronic gadgetry.

Doors

One of the most basic points for access control are doors, after all without a door there is no restricting who should or should not enter a building or a specific area within a building. Even the most complex of electronic access control systems still requires the use of doors. Two of the aspects relative to how efficient a door is at keeping out unwanted intruders are the quality of the doors and the locks that are fitted to them. The locks we will deal with separately in the next section. Doors should be divided into two security categories:-

External/Security doors - These are doors that are expected to prevent an unwanted intruder gaining access to a building, or part of a building. They may be subjected to a person trying to force access through them.

Internal Doors - These are doors which safeguard particular areas of a building rather than the whole building. When locked, they are still intended to prevent access by unauthorised personnel but are unlikely to be subjected to a person trying to force access through them.

Taking these two categories and the relevant expectations of the doors into consideration, it follows that external/security doors will need to be substantially more robust than internal ones. The exception to this is where internal doors are to be used as fire doors, whose purpose is to contain and prevent the spread of smoke and fire.

Internal doors are quite often hollow flush doors, commonly referred to as 'Egg Box' doors. These are doors that are constructed using two thin sheets of laminate spaced apart to give the door thickness by a wooden edge. The middle of the laminate sheets contains lightweight materials, such as cardboard separators, to make the door ridged. This is why it is not particularly difficult to smash through them using only a fairly heavy ram, such as a chair or fire extinguisher.

An external or security door on the other hand should be of solid wood or metal construction. If it is wood construction, even though solid, it may still be necessary to have the vulnerable side fitted with metal sheeting.

Where it is necessary to have windows in the doors, security glass, glass of extra thickness and strength, should always be used for external/security doors. Any hinges that are fitted to external/security doors should be fitted between the door frame and the edge of the door, so that they cannot be unscrewed without the door being in the open position.

Finally where windows are not fitted to external or security doors, it is always advisable to fit a good quality spy hole in the door. This enables anyone requiring access to be viewed for authorisation before the door is opened.

Locks

Having first ensured that the appropriate doors have been fitted it is then important to ensure that locks that are fitted to the door are of the right quality and standard. There are numerous makes and s of locks available on the market but before any are purchased it is always advisable to check with the business' insurers first. Some insurers insist on a particular make and specification in order to satisfy their insurance schedules.

Consideration should be given to whether traditional locks that require keys are to be used, or manual digital ones, that require a combination of numbers or letters or both (alpha numeric) to be entered into a keypad. If a digital lock is to be fitted to an external door it is usually a good idea to fit a conventional lock as well. This will enable the door to be fully 'locked down' when no one is working on the premises, therefore restricting access to even code holders and allowing access to just one or two essential key-holders.

Although there are advantages to using digital locks in that there are no keys to be lost or reproduced, the codes used to access them can become vulnerable. This is especially the case if authorised users pass them to unauthorised users, or authorised users are covertly observed entering the digits into the key pad. This potential problem can be averted in part by educating the users to the potential problems and regularly changing the codes.

Even if the users are security conscious and follow the security advice, it is always good practice to regularly change the codes anyway, as on some systems it is possible to work out what digits are being used from the dirty finger marks on the lock keypad. It usually follows that the better the quality of the lock, the more it is likely to cost. Manufacturers that produce locks for the top end of the market boast that the locks are supplied with tailor made keys that cannot be illegally reproduced, or additional keys cut.

As with digital locks there are potential security risks with conventional locks and keys as well. The obvious and most common problem is that keys get lost and/or end up in the wrong hands. In such a situation there is no alternative other than to replace the locks and reissue the keys, which even for small premises can be quite an expensive affair. Another problem with conventional locks that is becoming more of a cause for concern is that they can be 'bumped'. 'Bumping' is the process of adapting a similar make of key by filing it down to a particular size. It takes quite literally a couple of minutes to do, The key will then fit and operate all locks that are fitted with that particular make of key, the adapted key effectively becoming an unauthorised form of 'master key'.

Key management

Strict key and key code management is essential if the security of locks is not to be compromised. Central to effective physical key management has to be a well maintained key register. The key register should detail the key details, who signed them out and when they were returned. To accompany the register there should also be a list of who is authorised to draw keys out and on what basis i.e. on a temporary or permanent basis.

When deciding who keys should be issued to, thought should be given to 'Do they really need them?' and 'Can they be trusted with them?'. It could well be that it is not necessary for a person to have permanent possession of the keys. It may be sufficient for them to book the keys out for a specific period of time and then return them.

'Active keys', keys that are booked in and out on a regular basis, and spare keys should always be locked away in order to prevent them getting into the wrong hands. In addition they should be regularly audited to make sure that they are all accounted for. One fundamental security breach that is commonly overlooked is that keys should immediately be taken off individuals who are leaving the business, going on leave, are sick both long and short term, and most certainly anyone that is subject to suspension or dismissal.

Security Guards

The use of security guards is still by far the most popular and effective method of manual access control. One of the benefits of using security guards is that they provide the personal touch that other forms of access control cannot provide. More importantly, after a relatively short period of time, if the same security guard is always used, they get to know those who should be permitted access and those that should not. Without doubt a smartly turned out, polite and knowledgeable security guard can be an impressive asset to any business.

Unfortunately as much as this approach sounds like an ideal one, it can at times be a far from ideal solution. Firstly, unlike the outright purchase of other forms of access control, the use of security guards is an ongoing cost and quite an expensive one at that. There are also the potential added problems associated with sickness, holidays and general 'no shows.' Serious consideration should be given to the fact that in most cases the first point of contact with a business is the security guard. This may be an issue if the security guard is not smartly turned out, polite or knowledgeable and worse, is unreliable.

Electronic Access Control

The general principle of how any form of electronic access control operates is that a request for access will only be approved following the comparison of certain agreed credentials against a control list maintained on a database of some form. The methods used for the comparison can be made by a host or server, by an access control panel, or by a reader. A system usually operates along the lines of having a control panel as the centre of the system, which holds the data to be compared, connected to a number of readers located where the access is to be controlled and where the data is imputed for comparison.

Some recent technological developments are however, incorporating the control panel and reader functions together and placing them at the location where access is being requested. The latest controllers that are now available are Internet Protocol (IP) enabled, which means that they are not dependant on traditional controllers, but communicate directly to a computer host and database by utilising the facilities of standard computer networks.

There are numerous ways that access control readers can operate and they are classified by virtue of the functions that they are able to perform. The categories that they come under are:

Basic Non-Intelligent Readers – These at the present time are the most popular readers. The reader simply reads the card number or inputted PIN, following which it then forwards it to the control panel for verification.

Semi-Intelligent Readers – These are readers that have Input and Output facilities that can be used for functions relating to the door hardware, such as the locks, door contacts and exit buttons. These systems do not make any decisions, but operate by the information from the card or inputted PIN being sent to the main controller, whereupon it then waits for the controllers response. The potential problem with this system is that if the connection to the main controller is any way interrupted, the readers will only operate with limited functionality or stop working altogether.

Intelligent Readers – These readers also have all of the input and output means to control the door hardware, but are different from the non-intelligent and semi-intelligent systems in that they have memory and processing power that enable them to make independent access decisions. This is achieved as a result of the control panel sending and receiving configuration updates directly to and from the readers.

This latest technological innovation can provide readers with some useful additional features. These might include LCD and function buttons for data collection purposes such as clocking-in/clocking-out events to enable the production of time and attendance reports, and or camera/speaker/microphone functions in order to facilitate two-way intercom set-ups.

We'll now look at some of the benefits and drawbacks of implementing electronic access control systems to operate in conjunction with, or instead of, manual methods.

Security Doors

One of the most significant benefits of fitting an electronic access control system to a door, whether it is an external door allowing access to a building, or an internal door providing access to restricted or controlled areas, is that it provides an instant security barrier to the area that requires the protection. The protection that electronic access provide, despite the initial costs of installing it, can be far cheaper both in the short and most definitely the long term, than paying for a security guard or administrator to sit near the door and physically control who is allowed to pass through. This is especially so if there is more than one door that needs to be covered. This said, in instances where multiple doors are to be protected this is usually done by one person operating all of the electronic access from a central point, such as a reception area or security office.

One of the other benefits to be had from such a system is that irrespective of what specific system is installed, it will invariably incorporate an electronic log which will provide information as to who passed through it, when they passed through it, and how long it was before they passed back out of it. This kind of information can be invaluable, especially when conducting security investigations.

Before an electronic access system is fitted to a door consideration will need to be given to the construction and condition of the door. It is no use fitting a device to a door that would be easy enough to barge through, or if it is falling off its

hinges. Sometimes a standard door can be easily improved just by having metal sheeting fitted to the outside face and a good quality door closer installed. The final potential weak spot will be the types of locks that are fitted to the door that will be operated by the system. These need to be of the best quality that the budget will allow. Finally, if the budget will allow, it is best to have the door covered by CCTV, as it can provide an additional level of security, the reasons for which will become apparent in the next section.

Irrespective of how 'Hi Tec' the electronic access system is, they are still prone to some very fundamental security risks. One of the most common is unauthorised intrusion. This can be achieved in a number of ways:

By leaving the electronic Access Door open. This situation normally takes place when doors have been wedged open, usually with the aid of a nearby fire extinguisher, in order to allow a delivery to be made, or for ventilation on a hot day.

By following an authorised user through the door, sometimes referred to by the nickname 'Tailgating'. Although 'Tailgating' can sometimes occur without the knowledge of the authorised user, in that the door may be of the type that closes slowly behind the authorised user, allowing the unauthorised person time to slip through behind them before it shuts, it is however, more likely to take place as a result of the authorised user deliberately holding the door open for the unauthorised user, quite often as an act of politeness.

If the electronic access control is fitted to a door, as opposed to other entry means, then this particular type of potential security breach can be significantly reduced security awareness training for those using the system, or by operator intervention. Operator intervention will inevitably mean the implementation of additional security measures, such as a security vestibule, sometimes referred to as a 'Mantrap' or 'Air lock'. This approach is usually only encountered in high level security situations and works by firstly allowing the authorised user to gain access to a separate secure area. Here they are held and subjected to scrutiny by a CCTV operator or receptionist checking access authorisation. Only when identification and authorisation checks are satisfied will the CCTV operator allow the person to pass through a second secure door to gain access to the actual area they are authorised to visit.

By levering the door open. Levering the door open can sound quite extreme but can be quite simple to do by an implement like a screwdriver or jemmy and is an effective way of gaining unauthorised access. This can be particularly so if the fabric of the door or electronic locking system are of inferior quality and are not fitted with forced door monitoring alarms. Even where forced door monitoring systems are in place their effectiveness can sometimes be questionable, especially if they are prone to signalling false alarms or where there are no investigating alarm activations whether they be false or genuine.

By bypassing the electronic access system altogether – This method can be no more complicated than climbing through an open ground floor window. However, access can also be easily achieved in locations that are not located on a ground floor but where the construction of the walls are made out of non-solid materials. Commonly referred to as 'stud walls' they are frequently encountered in shared office blocks, or smaller restricted areas within a substantially constructed location such as a cash office for example. In such a situation the process is quite simple, crash through the wall. Although in some cases this can be easily achieved by using bare hands and body weight as a battering ram, a sledge hammer will most definitely be a more than adequate tool for quickly making a hole big enough to pass through.

Overriding the electronic locks- Once again a very simple method of gaining unauthorised access to a protected area and not as noisy or messy as crashing through a wall. This method can be achieved in several ways. For instance, the use of a strong magnet such as those commonly used in conjunction with Electronic Article Surveillance (EAS) Systems. The principle behind this method is that the magnet interferes with the solenoid controlling the bolts in the electric locking hardware. If the power source to the electronic access control system is interfered with, by either reducing or enhancing the current, or a power surge to the electronic locks is generated, it can cause the lock to malfunction and open. This is particularly so where such systems have been designed so that if they fail, they fail with the locks in the open position. This function is usually designed for the purposes of dealing with emergency situations such as fires and power cuts so that people do not become trapped as a result of the locks failing to open.

Before any form of electronic access control system is installed a comprehensive risk assessment and cost benefit analysis should be conducted to establish whether such an approach is the best one for the business.

Electronic Keys

As the name would suggest electronic keys are keys that operate electronic locks. Unlike conventional keys that always look like what they are, an electronic key can take a number of guises. This is because unlike a conventional key that physically opens a mechanical lock, an electronic key generally does not do so. They are instead presented to an electronic reader, which transmits the information contained on the card, usually the persons ID, to a database. If the information matches that which is held on the database, in that the key holder is authorised to pass that point, the reader will signal the electronic lock to open.

Most electronic keys are in the form of a card, pretty similar in dimensions to a credit card, but quite often slightly thinner, or in the form of a key fob, of various shapes, sizes and colours.

As to whether or not a card or fob is used in conjunction with the reader depends on a number of considerations, these are:-

The environment in which the electronic keys are to be used - key fobs are generally more robust than cards, so are ideal to attach to key rings and place in pockets or bags. In some cases, particularly in manufacturing locations it would be a Health & Safety risk to carry an electronic key on a lanyard around the neck or attached to clothing.

Who are the intended users of the electronic keys? - If the users of the keys are office based workers, then cards may be more appropriate, especially if the cards double as a visible form of identification.

Whether it will be used for any other functions? - Some electronic keys are used for a number of functions in addition to access control, such as for use with vending machines. It is therefore essential that there is parity between all of the electronic readers and electronic keys.

Advantages of Electronic Keys

The advantages of using electronic keys is that as soon as the decision is made to deny an electronic key holder access, it is quite simply a question of removing their details from the information database. Except for the cost of having to keep replacing the fobs or cards, it is not essential to repossess them as would be the case with a conventional key, thereby saving costs of having new keys cut.

Disadvantages of Electronic Keys

Irrespective of which electronic key system is opted for it should be remembered that, as with conventional keys, electronic keys can be compromised. One of the most common but nevertheless sophisticated forms of attack is where 'hackers' use portable scanners to capture the information held on the cards or fobs. This information can then be used on an illegally manufactured key to deceive the electronic reader and gain access. This method of compromising electronic keys is made easier by virtue of the fact that the information held on the card is not in any way encrypted.

Turnstiles and Barriers

When trying to decide whether to fit turnstiles or security barriers at a location it is first necessary to consider the type of location that you are proposing to place them in. What do you expect them to do?

Turnstiles

Older turnstiles are very large devices, much larger than an average size door, both in height and in width dimensions. They comprise a rotating set of horizontal bars that basically form a kind of rotating door. The bars are spaced fairly close together, so that even the smallest of children cannot climb through them.

Turnstiles were originally designed to operate as a manual device but are now also available fitted with electronic access control. For the purpose of this section we will be examining only the electronic versions.

When fitted to electronic turnstiles, the rotating horizontal bars can be set so that they rotate in either one direction only, or in both directions. This is so that they can be set to allow people to pass through them in one direction only, perhaps in order to force them to exit the location in a different area, or because there are barriers positioned next to each other for allowing dedicated entrance and exit only.

The barriers are usually set to electronically and mechanically operate in both directions if there is insufficient room to install separate barriers for the purpose of dedicated entrance and exit, or in order to accommodate high volumes of people requiring entrance and egress to a site throughout the day and possibly night. For electronic turnstiles to work properly they will need to be fitted with an electronic access control system. In order for an individual to pass through the turnstile they will need to present their electronic key to the electronic reader. Once the information on the electronic key has been verified against a database, the horizontal bars will release from a locked position allowing the person to push through them to enter or exit the controlled area.

Irrespective of which make of electronic access control is fitted to the turnstiles, it must be capable of being programmed with an 'anti-pass back' facility. The 'anti-pass back' facility is designed to prevent a situation whereby a person passes through the turnstile and then passes the electronic key back through the bars to another person, allowing them unauthorised access. With an 'anti-pass back' programme installed the electronic key will not allow another access because it has not received a request for an exit first. In other words an attempt has been made for two entries, without an exit being registered in between.

Like most security systems there is always a way around a problem. In the case of turnstiles fitted with anti-pass back, the method is quite simply to firstly pass through the turnstile, once authorised to do so, and then present the key to the electronic reader on the other side, once authorisation to exit has been approved, spin the horizontal bars in the exit direction without stepping into them, then pass the card back as normal, thus fooling the system that an entry, followed by an exit, has been made before another entry authorisation has been requested. There are two ways that this situation can be prevented. Firstly install additional software onto the database that will allow it to produce exception reports of suspicious activity, such as numerous entrance/exits in a short period of time, or install CCTV cameras in order to monitor the use of the turnstiles.

Although turnstiles can be fitted inside premises, because of their size they are generally installed outside buildings, normally on the perimeter of the premises. Because turnstiles are a robust form of access control and will withstand most forms of attempt to damage them, they are normally used for such locations as manufacturing sites or warehouse facilities.

Finally if it is decided that turnstiles are to be used for access control, then provisions will also have to be made for disabled access. Usually this is in the form of a separate electronic access controlled gate located between a pair of turnstiles or at the side of one of them. This gate can also be of benefit for a person wishing to gain access that is carrying a large item, as they will not be able to fit through the turnstiles. For obvious reason this gate will need to be carefully monitored as it could be prone to abuse. It is important that measures are put in place so that neither the turnstiles, nor the gate can be bypassed by climbing over them, or by passing either side of them.

Security barriers

Security barriers operate in exactly the same way as turnstiles. The only differences between the two systems is that security barriers are considerably smaller, normally not much taller than waist height and they do afford the same level of security in terms of access control. For these reasons security barriers are normally installed in locations where they can be physically monitored, for instance in an underground railway station or in reception areas of office complexes.

The principle behind security barriers is that they provide a sufficient and appropriate level of security to allow authorised individuals access to a controlled location, without the level of security being too severe. Where such barriers are fitted in office complexes, you are hardly likely to see the CEO's PA climbing over the barriers because she has forgotten her electronic key.

Electronic Access Control Management

The benefits of using electronic access control systems is that in addition to the automated security control that they provide, the information that the systems generate can be used for other purposes. It cannot be stressed enough that any electronic access control system that is installed should be compliant with the latest fire and Health & Safety regulations, in respect of how they should operate in the event of an emergency. Once they have been configured to operate in conjunction with the regulations they will need to be regularly serviced and inspected to ensure that they are still operating properly.

ID Cards

Providing that they are used properly the use of ID cards can be a simple and effective way of controlling both access to, and within certain restricted areas of a business. The most common form of ID card is the 'self-completed' that is used to register visitors to a location.

The 'self-completed' is where a visitor is requested to complete a carbonated form on which they provide their personal details, the details of their vehicle if they have parked on the premises and the details of the person they are visiting. The top copy is then detached and displayed in a clear wallet which they are then expected to display. The visitor pass, as they are sometimes called, should be clearly marked with the word 'VISITOR' and the date. The pass is usually only valid for one day.

This process can be quite effective in the event that the premises have to be evacuated as the carbonated details can be used as an additional role call register to ensure that not only have the permanent staff been evacuated from the premises but the visitors have also been accounted for. In addition, whilst the individual is on the premises they are effectively labelled as being a visitor and not a regular member of the staff, which can alert regular members of staff if the visitor is found in areas of the business that they should not be.

Where this process frequently beaks down is when the visitor fails to return their portion of the form before vacating the premises, staff do not take enough notice of individuals wearing passes, and the visitor continues to use their pass to come and go as they please. This bad security practice can easily be rectified by making the person the visitor is calling on responsible for escorting them around the premises at all times and ensuring they leave the pass at the reception desk before leaving.

We'll now take a look at more sophisticated types of ID cards and how they can best be utilised.

Picture ID Cards

Because of the cost implications and the time normally spent producing them, picture ID Cards, that is to say an ID card bearing the picture of the person that it has been issued to, are normally only issued to members of staff that are permanently based at a particular location. The ID card must be worn in a prominent position by the person that it has been issued to, normally on a lanyard around the neck, or on a clip on the trousers/skirt waistband, so that it can easily be viewed by other members of staff and, if necessary, the security team.

On larger business premises the background of the ID card or lanyard can be colour coded to denote access levels that holder of the ID card may have. An example of this method would be in relation to high security areas, such as cash offices or computer network rooms. It would not be desirable to allow all members of staff to have easy access to these areas but the members of staff that are expected to access them could have an ID card with a red background, or have the ID card attached to a red lanyard.

Electronic ID Cards

The principles of the electronic ID card are quite simply a combination of the principles of an electronic key, which was covered earlier in the section, and those of a photo ID Card. The obvious benefit of this system is that the ID cards can be individually programmed for each person, authorising them access to only specific areas of the business where they need to be.

ID Card Management

How successful an ID card system will be is dependent on how well it is managed. The tighter the controls concerning their issue and use, the more effective the chosen system will be. Unfortunately the wearing of ID Cards in some businesses and organisations can have adverse effects in that some members of staff do not like wearing them at all for all sorts of reasons.

The most common excuse for not wearing them is that they breach Health and Safety regulations, which as mentioned earlier is a fair point if the individual is working in a potentially dangerous environment, or in one where food is produced. In an office situation this excuse is a little thin. However it can easily be eliminated by issuing ID card holders that attach to clothing or are worn on an armband, or by using quick release lanyards for those that have a fear of being choked to death.

In other businesses and organisations the wearing of an ID card can be viewed as a status symbol, especially when the ID cards are issued for different levels of access. This situation can result at times in almost child-like behaviour, with individuals demanding that they be issued with an ID card of a certain level because they are senior to so and so, or have been with the business longer. Pressure to issue ID cards under these circumstances should not be tolerated.

Where business and organisations have implemented an ID card system then it should be firmly enforced with disciplinary procedures being considered for persistent offenders who fail to wear them or even bring them to work. As most businesses display their Company Logo on ID cards, they should not be worn outside the business premises but put somewhere safe until they are used again. This will avoid potential situations whereby the individual may be compromised by would be criminals in some way.

Biometrics

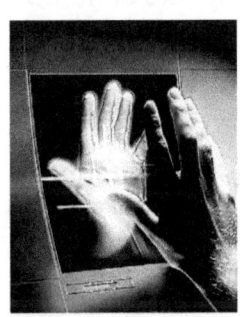

The term biometrics refers to any means by which a person can be uniquely identified by one or more distinguishing biological traits. At first glance it would be presumed that this is a relatively new subject to be associated with the general security industry, but it is not be any means. One of the oldest methods of biometric verification techniques that everyone is familiar with is fingerprinting.

Although Sir Francis Galton is credited with making the use of fingerprints an acceptable form of evidence in criminal courts, it was perhaps Sir William Hershel who pioneered the use of fingerprinting as a biometric verification, on the tea plantations in India during the 1850's. Hershel, concerned with an increasing problem that some workers on the plantations were being paid twice for their labours and some not at all, introduced a system whereby the workers had to place a thumb print at the side of their name when collecting their wages. This could then be authenticated against fingerprints held on file by the pay clerks.

In addition to fingerprinting, other ways by which a person can be uniquely identified through biometric verification include; retina and Iris patterns in the eye, DNA, earlobe geometry, hand geometry and complete face recognition. In order to understand what makes biometric verification techniques work it is first necessary to understand the specific aspects of human characteristics that can be used. These aspects can be placed into seven categories. They are:-

>1. **Universality** - Each person must have the same type of human characteristic in order that comparisons can be made between them.
>
>2. **Uniqueness** - The human characteristic that is to be the subject of biometric comparison needs to be almost if not totally unique to the individual in order to distinguish them from other individuals.
>
>3. **Permanence** - The characteristic needs to be permanent. It should not be subject to natural change as a result of the human ageing process, or by forced changes. An example of the latter is where criminals

have unsuccessfully attempted to remove their fingerprint ridges by burning them off with acid. Older habitual burglars often had scarred finger tips, having cut them with a blade to prevent sufficient points of recognition from being identified.

4. **Collectable** - The characteristics have to be easily measured or compared. It would not be practical for instance, to base biometric verification on the size of an individual's kidney.

5. **Performance** - The technology used to measure the biometric characteristics will need to be fast, accurate, robust and easy to use.

6. **Acceptability** - Before biometric verification methods of any description can be used they will first need to be accepted at levels as a reliable comparing human characteristics. The level of acceptance will vary depending on what the technology is being used for. A good and fairly recent example of this is in relation to DNA profiling. Before such technology was allowed to be used as admissible evidence in a Court of Law the technology had to be approved by the House of Lords.

7. **Circumvention** - How successful a biometric system of any type is will ultimately be dependent on how easy it is to circumvent by substitution. As with any technology

that is implemented to provide security, there will always be individuals trying to develop ways to compromise it.

A biometric system can be used for two purposes, these being Identification and verification. We will now take a look at the requirements for each of these categories:-

- **Identification** - For identification purposes one known biometric characteristic is compared with other known biometric characteristics that have already been captured on the biometric database. The identification of an individual will only succeed if the characteristic submitted for comparison matches the template on the database, provided that it falls within a previously set threshold.

- **Verification** -   The process of using biometrics for verification purposes is a fairly straightforward one in that is purely a comparison of a biometric characteristic of an individual with a characteristic of that individual that has already been stored on a database template.

Irrespective of the type of biometric system that is to be used, fingerprint, iris recognition etc., the general operating process will always be the same. Before an individual can successfully use the chosen system they will have to go through a process called 'enrolment'. To explain this in simplistic terms, the process is no different in some respects to guests being allowed into an invitation only party. First, before they are allowed admission, their invitations will be checked against their names that have already been provided and held on a guest list at the door. Only if their names on the invitations match the names that appear on the guest list will they be let in. If not they will be refused entry.

With a biometric system information will need to be captured from an individual, in the form of biometric characteristics, whereupon it will then be stored either on a database or card. When the individual subsequently uses the system their biometric characteristics will again be captured but then compared with those already held on the database as a result of the 'enrolment'. Only if the two sets of biometric characteristics match will the person's identity be confirmed and they will be allowed access.

As is invariably the case with all new forms of technology it can be expensive and unreliable. This was the case with the early generations of biometric systems that incorporated fingerprint and iris recognition methods. This is now not the case, with systems being a lot more affordable, quick and reliable. However, when choosing a system careful consideration should still be given to the manufacturers claimed performance. It does not always follow that the more you pay the better the system will be and vice versa.

A more scientific approach to judging the performance of a biometric system is by analysing the individual performance metrics. These are categorised in the following way:

The False Acceptance Rate (FAR) or False Match Rate (FMR) - This is quite simply where the system is judged by how many incorrect matches are made between the characteristics that are inputted and the characteristics that are held on the database or card. What you are looking for in terms of FAR or FMR results is the percentage level of incorrectly matched inputs, obviously the lower the percentage figure the better the overall performance should be.

The False Reject Rate (FRR) or False Non-Match Rate (FNMR) - This is the process of examining the probability of the system incorrectly failing to establish a match between the characteristics that are inputted and the characteristics that are already held on the database. What is being looked for in this case is the percentage of valid inputted characteristics that are incorrectly rejected.

The Receiver/Relative Operating Characteristic (ROC) - Although a little more technical to deal with than the previous two categories, the ROC is basically an acceptance that things will not always be 100% correct, so allows for an agreed and permitted tolerance between the FAR and the FRR. The system will take this agreed tolerance into consideration when trying to determine a match of inputted and held characteristics, before acknowledging them as a match or not. Logic then follows in that the higher the agreed tolerance then the fewer non-matches there will be. The lower the agreed tolerance the more it will reduce the FAR but increase the FRR.

The Equal Error Rate (EER) or Crossover Error Rate (CER) - This is quite simply the rate for which accept and reject errors occur in equal numbers. Without going into the physics of how this figure is calculated, it is only necessary to know that the lower the EER, the more accurate the system is likely to be.

The Failure to Enrol Rate (FER or FTE) – Is the rate of attempts to enter an individual's biometric characteristics onto a database, that are unsuccessful. This problem can sometimes be caused as a result of a failure on the part of the equipment used to read the characteristics, but is more likely to be as a result of poor quality inputs. This is therefore a difficult area to judge in terms of performance.

Failure to Capture Rate (FTC) – This is perhaps one of the most important aspects of a biometric system to consider. If a system regularly fails to detect the inputted characteristics, then its suitability should seriously be reconsidered.

The Database Capacity (DC) – How much characteristic data can be stored on a particular system is quite often relative to the size and overall cost of the system, based on what the system is likely to be expected to do. Careful thought should be applied when deciding on the size of a system, particularly when planning for long term usage. Small capacity systems may not be a suitable option for the following reasons:-

(i) The business is likely to continue to grow, in terms of personnel size.

(ii) There is a possibility of separate business divisions coming together and integrating with the system.

(iii) There is a possibility of the business joining with other business, perhaps as a result of an acquisition.

Fingerprint Recognition

Perhaps one of the oldest forms of biometric methods to be used is fingerprint recognition. As mentioned earlier, Sir William Hershel recognised that each fingerprint was different, but it was Sir Francis Galton who actually defined the different characteristics of a fingerprint. These are referred to as the Galton Points. In order to accommodate further advancements associated with fingerprint technology, the Galton Points were defined further and referred to as a subset called minutiae points.

Fingerprint characteristics are divided into three main groups of print pattern ridges. They are;-

- **Arches** - An arch is a pattern where the ridges enter from one side of the finger, rise in the centre forming an arc, and then exit on the other side of the finger.

- **Loops** - The loop is a pattern where the ridges enter from one side of a finger, form a curve, and tend to exit from the same side as they enter.

- **Whorls** - In the whorl pattern, ridges form circularly around a central point on the finger.

When fingerprints are developed, that is to say fingerprint ink is applied to the tip of a finger and then it is pressed onto a sheet of paper, the highest part of the ridge is defined as a black line and the valleys in between the ridges appear as a blank space. The analysis of fingerprints in order to establish a match between prints requires the identical comparison of several features within the print patterns.

The analysis of fingerprints was originally a totally manual affair in that it was carried out by fingerprint experts who were trained to recognise the different characteristics of fingerprints and then give an expert opinion as to whether they were a match or not. Most fingerprint analysis now is conducted using electronic technology that compares the fingerprints in two ways; by comparing the ridges or by comparing the complete pattern. It is this technology that is now used in conjunction with biometric access control systems.

In order to use fingerprints on a biometric access control system, instead of the fingerprints being developed by using ink they are actually read by placing the fingers on a fingerprint sensor, which captures a digital image of the fingerprint pattern. The first time a fingerprint is captured on a system it is used for enrolment purposes and thereafter is used for matching purposes. Depending on the type of fingerprint sensor being used the comparisons are made by comparing specific ridges, or by comparing the complete pattern

Fingerprint scanning can be used for additional purposes other than gaining access through doors. This form of technology is becoming more frequently used within the banking sector to access accounts. Some schools are now using it for pupil registration and to allow pupils to withdraw funds from parent financed accounts in order to pay for school meals etc. Fingerprint technology is even being used in airports to speed up immigration processes.

Advantages

The advantages of using this type of technology is that the process of identifying individuals by their fingerprint patterns is a tried, tested and reliable process which, to date, no one has been able to discredit.

Disadvantages

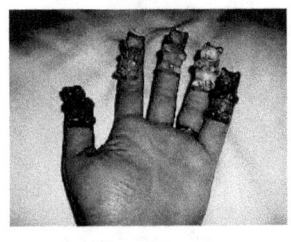

The potential disadvantages of using this technology is that in some circumstances, where individuals are not monitored at the time fingerprints are presented to the fingerprint scanners, there is always an opportunity to present false information. This could be in the form of falsely presenting the fingerprints of another person that have in some way been taken and developed without their knowledge. In very extreme cases, as horrible as it may sound, another person's amputated finger has been used to deceive the technology.

Fingerprint scanners have also been subject to a variety of bypass methods. These range from people lifting latent prints from the scanner and using them as their own, to making replica fingerprints from gelatine which has very similar capacitance to human skin. Many people have damaged finger ridges and it will not be possible to identify such persons using fingerprint scanners. Although there are very valid reasons why such damage might have occurred, loss prevention specialists should be aware that, for some time, habitual burglars deliberately damaged the tips of their fingers by either scarring them or using acid on them so that they did not leave legally admissible fingerprints at the scenes of their crimes.

Iris Recognition

The process of using iris recognition is not too dissimilar to the process of identifying people by fingerprint patterns. This is because, like fingerprint patterns, it has been proved that a person's iris patterns are unique to that individual and so therefore they can be identified by them.

This form of biometric technology works as a result of the eye being placed against a scanner. The iris is illuminated with infrared light to enhance the patterns of the iris that are then recorded by a digital image onto a database.

Advantages

There are numerous advantages to using this type of biometric technology over any other, they are:

- The technology is not affected by individuals who wear contact lenses or glasses.

- The eye is technically an internal organ, so is in the main well protected against damage.

- Unless there is at some point a severe injury caused to the eye, enrolment can last a lifetime.

- Unlike fingerprint ridges that can actually deteriorate in quality the iris patterns only deteriorate through disease.

- The technology has an unprecedented false match rate.
- Contrary to belief, iris patterns can be read from distances ranging from approximately 10cm to a couple of metres away, so there is no need for an individual to touch scanning equipment.

Disadvantages

There are several disadvantages to using iris scanning technology:

- It is still a relatively new form of technology and for that reason it means that it is still fairly expensive to buy when compared with other systems.
- It is no different to other forms of biometric technologies in that it can be prone to recognition issues, mainly due to having to operate with poor quality images.
- It is no different to other forms of biometric technologies, in particular fingerprint recognition in that it cannot distinguish between live and dead tissue. This allows individuals to design templates showing another person's iris details to present to the readers. This could be achieved by presenting a very high quality photograph or some form of fake eye.

Iris pattern and more lately retina pattern biometric authentication methods are increasingly being used in airports and at bank Automatic Teller Machines (ATM's).

Facial Recognition

The use of facial recognition technology has been around for quite a while now. In fact it came into being not long after the introduction of digital CCTV systems. It was initially used by the police as a reliable identifying known trouble makers in football crowds and prolific shoplifters when they entered CCTV monitored town centres.

The fundamental way this technology works is to compare digital CCTV images or video frames with an existing video source. Positive comparisons are achieved as a result of analysing specific facial features with those held on a database. Examples of the facial features that are usually analysed include; the position, size and or shape of eyes, nose, cheekbones and jaw, which is called a geometric approach and provides a match based on distinguishing features. Another approach for identifying individuals is the photometric approach; this technology distils an image into algorithmic values and produces a match by eliminating any variances with the images of those already held on a database.

The latest facial recognition systems now use three dimensional (3D) technologies which makes the process of identification significantly more accurate. This enables comparisons of the shape and contours of the face to be made. Unlike other facial recognition systems the benefit of using 3D systems is that they are not in any way affected by changes in lighting conditions and they can operate by viewing a profile from a number of different angles.

If automatic facial recognition images are to be used to match images that have been captured and stored on a database, then both images should be of a sufficient standard to ensure an accurate match. Irrespective of how accurate an automatic facial recognition system is at establishing matches between images, procedures should be put in place to ensure that all automatic matches are also verified by a human operator. The human operator having assessed an automatic match and concurred with the findings will then be in a position to decide what action should be taken. For compliance and audit trail purposes, details of the assessment conducted by the human operator should be recorded and kept on file. This should be the case whether a match was established or not.

Advantages

The advantages of using biometric systems like these become obvious:-

- The system can be installed to detect shoplifters or individuals known for assaulting retail staff.

- The system can be linked to other similar systems operated by other retailers or the police, therefore significantly enlarging the database gallery of known or suspected offenders.

- It removes the problem of the security guards having to be able to see and/or identify known offenders. This is of particular importance when different security guards, not familiar with the local personalities, are used.

- Network databases that are linked to it will also identify known or suspected offenders that are operating away from their usual or 'home' areas.

Disadvantages

The disadvantages of using facial recognition systems are:-

- Cost. Once again one of the potential disadvantages of using this technology is the expense involved. As is always the case, the systems are becoming cheaper to purchase as the technology gets older and more manufacturers produce them.

- Experienced criminals can circumnavigate identification by changing or covering their faces, which can even fool 3D systems.

Biometric Management

Irrespective of the type of biometric system that is to be used it is imperative that careful consideration should be given to as to whether the chosen system will be 'up to the job' in more ways than one.

Systems that are purchased for operation in a warehouse environment will need to be more robust in terms of construction, circumnavigation, and possible abuse than a system that is purchased for use in an office block. Databases that store the information necessary to make the system function will need to be of an appropriate size and relatively complex in respect of the functions that they will be expected to perform.

Although one of the disadvantages of implementing a biometric system is cost, the financial impact to a business may be somewhat softened in some circumstances if the system is carefully managed so as to incorporate a number of different and beneficial functions. Some of the functions that could be incorporated within such systems can include:-

- Having them linked to the Company pay role, as part of the clocking on/off process, especially in cases where workers are hourly paid.

- Linking them to the Personnel/HR department, so that time and attendance statistics can be compiled and monitored.

- Using the data to generate accurate fire evacuation registers

- Interfacing them with cashless vending equipment.

- Incorporating them with cashless payment systems for items purchased in staff canteens/Company shops etc.

Finally, operating procedures for individuals using the systems will need to be formulated and in some cases consultation prior to their installation will be required between representatives of the business and trade union representatives. Contingency plans for an alternative operation should also be compiled, in order to cover the eventuality of a full or partial system failure.

Chapter 3

Closed Circuit Television (CCTV)

Most people by now have heard of CCTV and understand the basic reasons it exists. One of the main applications of CCTV systems is for the protection of property, however there are other applications that CCTV can be used for such as:-

- Assisting production managers to control the flow of work, identify production 'bottlenecks' and take corrective action.

- Monitoring in hostile or sterile environments which may not ordinarily be accessible by a human being, such as automated food processing locations or furnaces.

In this section we will look at the different CCTV systems that are available and explore the possibilities of when, where, to what extent and under what circumstances such systems could be used. At the end of the section we will take a detailed look at the UK legislation that must be complied with if a CCTV system is to be, or already has been, installed on business premises.

CCTV Selection

The term 'closed circuit derived from the fact that the cameras, monitors and or recording devices communicate across a proprietary cable and have no externally broadcasting signals of images that they are generating. With the advent of modern technology this has changed somewhat in that point to point wireless links between cameras and monitors are now commonly installed, using transmission such as microwave, but unlike broadcast television, which provided you have the right aerial, anyone can intercept, a CCTV signal is still not openly transmitted. To all intents and purposes it is still a form of closed circuit, albeit a high tech one.

Be aware, however, that technology is moving extremely quickly. It is now possible to purchase an App for an iPhone or iPad which allows someone to monitor a CCTV system from the other side of the world through the internet. Any internet based system can be 'hacked' and for this reason no CCTV system using this kind of technology should be considered totally secure.

The primary purpose of CCTV is to identify people, places and things. It is commonly used for surveillance purposes and generally comprises:

- cameras to view the subject;
- a recording device to store the information viewed by the cameras;

- A monitor or monitors to watch both what is being viewed by the camera and or being played back from the recording /storage device.

Key to the effectiveness of any CCTV system is the strategic placement of cameras and astute observation of the images that are relayed from the cameras to the monitors.

As mentioned at the beginning of this section, there are numerous situations where CCTV monitoring can be utilised. Within the loss prevention and risk management industry however, it is primarily installed for the purposes of;

- Detecting and observing intruders
- Allowing access to restricted areas
- Observing individuals who may pose a threat to the organisation
- Reduction of theft from such locations as retail premises and places of work

CCTV systems can also be used to help to detect fraud e.g. when it is used in conjunction with ATM's. Ultimately images that have been recorded properly and lawfully with these purposes in mind should be of a standard that enables them to be accepted in a court or tribunal as admissible evidence.

As the use of CCTV systems has become more widespread, particularly in the United Kingdom where there are reputed to be more cameras per person than anywhere else in the world, so have concerns for an individual's right to privacy under the Human Rights Act. So much so that legislation has been introduced in many countries to regulate the use of CCTV, particularly in relation to the data recorded by CCTV systems. In the case of the United Kingdom this legislation is the Data Protection Act (DPA) 1998, the full implications of which are covered at the end of this section.

Originally CCTV systems were mainly purchased and used by commercial or Government organisations. However, as CCTV systems have become cheaper to buy and more easily available they have become more widely used, even within the home. When considering the feasibility of using a CCTV system as a security tool for a business, it should not be considered as an automatic option purely because it is affordable and is expected because everyone else has got one. It is important to establish what the benefits for such an installation would be and whether those benefits or even greater benefits could be realised by other, less expensive and less intrusive means. An example of this would be using electronic article surveillance (EAS) technology to protect items of clothing instead of the clothing being monitored by CCTV cameras.

How CCTV systems work is not of great importance to the loss prevention and loss prevention specialist – that is knowledge required by CCTV installers and maintenance personnel. What the loss prevention and loss prevention specialist must know is what system to purchase to achieve the objectives set for the system. They must also ensure the CCTV Operators are sufficiently knowledgeable to be able to get the most benefit from the system. The operators are normally security guards, either contract or in-house, and for any CCTV system to be effective the operator must be properly trained.

CCTV System Components

There are tens of thousands of different models of the components that make up a CCTV system and they can be sourced globally. Although the cheapest tend to be from places like China, be aware that China manufactures electronic goods in 2 different formats, CE and non-CE for different markets. Only those carrying the CE mark may be used in Europe.

The basics of any CCTV system will include the following:

Cameras – Hundreds of thousands of different makes and models of camera from thousands of different manufacturers. They come in all shapes and sizes and are either fixed or what are known as Pan, Tilt and Zoom (*commonly referred to as PTZ*).

Monitors – used to view images. Numbers of monitors will be dependent on the size of the control room, number of operators and complexity of the system. Most these days are flat screen but CTX monitors are still used in many control rooms.

Multiplexers – provide the ability to look at images from numerous cameras on one monitor screen. At the moment up to 64 images can be seen on one screen and each image can be isolated and enlarged if necessary to allow more detailed viewing of a particular camera image. The multiplexer itself looks a bit like a domestic dvd player.

Recording Device – normally a Digital Video Recorder (DVR) at the moment. Again there are thousands of different models of DVR. It is important to choose one which will allow the greatest degree of flexibility in relation to time-lapse recording and recording capacity needed to achieve the system objectives.

Signal Transmission System – this will differ depending on the system which has been installed. Some are 'hard-wired' requiring cables, others are wireless or internet based.

CCTV System

There are generally three types of CCTV system: analogue, digital and IP.

Analogue CCTV Systems

Analogue CCTV systems are mainly obsolete today, having been superseded by digital and IP CCTV systems. These will be discussed later. The only analogue systems still in use in the UK today are likely to have been installed many years ago and not updated since. They record images onto video tape on a Video Cassette Recorder (VCR). Newly installed systems will be either digital or IP and for that reason no further mention will be made of analogue systems.

Digital CCTV Systems

Digital CCTV systems are configured in roughly the same way as an analogue system, but use digital technology to compress the viewed images before sending them to a monitor, after which the images can be stored onto a hard drive instead of onto a video tape.

It is necessary to save images in a compressed format because saving uncompressed digital recordings, even on a CCTV dedicated system, takes up an enormous amount of hard drive space. Images on a digital system are stored on the system hard drive, although they can be downloaded onto discs or USB drives. The downloading of images onto discs is usually conducted in order to produce the images as evidence and not for routine storage.

Depending on the number of cameras and capacity of the hard drive it could be filled within a couple of hours. One of the down sides to compressing the images is that there is a slight deterioration in the quality of pictures when played back. If this should create a problem the solution could be to fit motion detectors to the cameras to reduce the amount of images that would need to be recorded. The next generation of CCTV, Internet Protocol (IP) cameras are now being marketed to deal with this problem.

IP CCTV Systems

IP cameras are still fairly new technology and therefore still quite expensive to buy. The payback is that they can capture images at a far greater resolution than previous technologies. This is particularly useful when images need to be enlarged for such purposes as reading vehicle registration plates. One of the main benefits of this system though is that it enables users to view the cameras through any internet connection or by 3G/4G mobile telephone technology, referred to as a TCP/IP connection.

Advantages of IP Systems

There are many more advantages to be gained by using this technology. They include:

- **The ability to use the system to communicate two-way audio, via a single network cable** - This has been successfully used in monitoring stations to inform intruders that the police are on their way, or by staff in petrol stations instructing customers how to use automated prepay pumps.

- **Higher resolution cameras** - Better quality images that can assist with identifying offences and the offenders.

- **Greater flexibility** – The cameras can be repositioned anywhere on an IP Network, this includes cameras that can now operate using wireless technology.

- **They can be programmed with analytical software** - This kind of programming is developing all the time and can include software that allows cameras to determine when something has been taken, or a person has been assaulted.

- **The ability to transmit telemetry commands** – PTZ cameras can be controlled remotely via the internet.

- **They afford greater security** – IP cameras provide a secure data transmission by authentication and encryption.

- **Remote accessibility** – Live images can be viewed from any computer anywhere in the world.

- **They can be cost effective** – Recent studies claim that in systems with less than 16 cameras, analogue technology is cheaper, between 16 and 32 cameras the cost is approximately equal, in excess of 32 cameras IP cameras are more cost effective. As IP technology will no doubt become cheaper with time, these ratios will also change. Consideration must also be given to the operational efficiency and standard of images which can be gained from using IP systems.

- **IP Cameras can function via wireless technology** – Similar to a computer obtaining wireless internet access, this is achieved by a Router.

- **They do not need a separate power supply to function** - The latest IP cameras have the ability to be powered over an Ethernet connection, referred to as PoE.

Disadvantages of IP Systems

As with any technology, no matter how many advantages there are to the latest innovations there will still always be some disadvantages. In the case of IP cameras when compared with other cameras these are:-

- **Cost** – At the present time IP cameras are still quite expensive when compared with, analogue cameras but it is fair to assume eventually this may not be the case. Analogue cameras are now becoming ever more difficult to source and this, combined with maintenance issues, should not be underestimated when sourcing a new system.

- **Standards** – Possibly because it is relatively new technology there is no overall standard of encoding. Different systems use different programming interfaces, which means that that the cameras have to match the recorder. This is similar to smartphone technology where the two dominant systems are either IOS or Android based – one does not work with the other. Eventually one system will probably emerge as dominant but it is unlikely that there will ever be a time when only one system is in use.

- **High network Bandwidths** – A typical camera can require 3 mb per second.

- **Potential Technical barriers** – IP cameras require network settings, router settings, port forwarding and an IP address. This is not a major problem in itself provided that assistance is available from the business IT department or the installer of the system has been trained in these matters. From experience however, it will usually involve both parties.

- **Internet Security** – With a basic analogue system that operates with video tapes there is no possibility of a third party accessing the system. This makes it a truly closed affair, which is not necessarily the case for IP systems that rely on the internet to communicate. As with all internet facilities, the system is vulnerable to hacking for malicious and criminal reasons. It is therefore imperative that the latest internet security measures are put into place and are regularly reviewed as to their capabilities.

CCTV Surveys

Before installing or upgrading a CCTV system of any size, a comprehensive CCTV survey should be undertaken. The purpose of the survey should be to answer the following questions or to produce a cost-benefit analysis:

1. Does the current system (If there is one) really need upgrading, or does it do the job it is required to do?

2. Is the installation of a new CCTV system really necessary? Can other methods of crime prevention and detection be utilised that would be just as or more effective?

3. Is it necessary to install a large expensive system, or would a small basic system be more than adequate?

4. Could the installation of a CCTV system be integrated with other functions, such as product protection, access control or fire safety?

5. Are there drawings of the proposed system, together with itemised specifications of all of the equipment to be used.

6. Can the financial expenditure of a CCTV system be justified?

7. Can the initial installation and ongoing maintenance costs of a CCTV system be afforded by the business?

8. What level of impact will a CCTV system have on peoples' privacy.

If as a result of conducting a comprehensive and truly objective CCTV survey, it is deemed that the installation of a CCTV system would benefit the business, then a copy of the CCTV survey document should be attached, along with a detailed cost/benefit analysis report, to an application for expenditure request.

Intelligent CCTV

Most if not all modern CCTV systems use high definition colour cameras that are capable of focusing on even the most minute of details. When these high quality images are then linked to computer systems that have been installed with the appropriate software, they can be used to perform a whole host of different functions.

One of the most useful applications for these advances in technology is that they can be used as a tool for CCTV users to assist them in complying with CCTV related legislation, such as the DPA 1998. Examples of this are the requirement to blur faces or create 'virtual walls', thus preventing camera images in certain areas such as changing rooms.

In addition to being used for these purposes and for the purpose of biometric identification, good quality CCTV images can be used to semi or completely automatically track people and objects. This technology is referred to as Video Content Analysis or VCA. We will now take a look at some of the applications that VCA technology can be used for.

Product Protection

Such is the sophistication of VCA technology that systems can now determine not only if an object is moving, but the size of the object, or whether the object is a human or a vehicle. Some systems can even determine the colour of an object.

Software is available that uses this analysis to evaluate how a person moves and changes shape. This means that they can potentially determine when a person is loitering near monitored products, or if an item is placed in a pocket or inside a coat which might change a person's overall shape, instead of a trolley or store basket. VCA systems also provide the facility to place an individual on a virtual map, by calculating their position  from the CCTV images provided. It is then possible to place automatic tracking on that individual whilst they remain within a building or other areas covered by the CCTV cameras. This is a useful application to have in order to monitor suspected shoplifters, without the complication of trying to monitor them manually.

Cash Protection

VCA technology can really be advantageous when it is deployed to protect cash. Increasingly cameras are now being located above tills to monitor all till transactions because VCA technology can immediately identify when transactions are not being conducted properly. It is possible for example, to detect incidents where cash is taken from the customer by the till operator and placed under the till drawer, to be taken by the operator at a later time, instead of the cash being placed inside the drawer. This application is also useful for detecting the fraudulent use of loyalty and payment cards by staff members, and deliberate failure to scan goods when operating in conjunction with a relative, or friend.

Similar successes have been achieved where this system has been placed inside cash offices, or areas where safes are located. Once again individuals have been apprehended as a result of these systems detecting unnatural movement, such as placing money into pockets, underwear, personal bags etc.

Staff/ Public Protection

The implementation of VCA technology has had a major impact on how CCTV images are viewed. In some cases there is no longer a requirement for an operator to sit for hours watching banks of monitors. This is because cameras that are connected to VCA technology are not directly observing individuals but instead are monitoring their behaviour, specific movements, type of clothes they wear or bags that they may be carrying.

There is now VCA technology available that can identify potential cases of violent activity before an incident has taken place. This is achieved as a result of VCA systems being programmed to expect certain physical events to occur in a particular way. If a physical event occurs in a way that was not expected, it immediately becomes the subject of an electronic exception report, possibly allowing time for human intervention. An example of how this technology could be applied would be in relation to a customer becoming abusive with a checkout operator. As the customer becomes more agitated and aggressive their body language would change from the norm, in that their normal stance would change and they would perhaps start to wave their arms about. At this juncture the system would flag up an exception report allowing for the speedy intervention of another member of staff or a security guard.

Owing to the fact that VCA CCTV systems can be networked with other VCA systems, possibly operated by the police or other retailers, and that they are able to recognise specific individuals by virtue of what they wear or what they are carrying, this information can be used to identify a person as soon as they enter the retail premises. This provides the opportunity to immediately evict them or involve the police.

Automatic Number Plate Recognition (ANPR)

ANPR, is technology that was originally designed for and used exclusively by the police for the detection of wanted criminals and stolen vehicles. Nowadays it is used in a variety of situations from identifying vehicles approaching sensitive premises to tracking the amount of time a vehicle remains in a car park.

ANPR technology has also been used to combat the increasing problem of the theft of fuel from filling stations, commonly referred to as 'Drive Offs'. 'Drive Offs' initially became a problem for retailers with the introduction of self-service fuel pumps but has since become a problem of epic proportions due to the high value of fuel. Some individuals realised that they could make more money in one 'Drive Off' than they could earn by doing a full day of work in a low paid job. This was particularly so when they not only filled the vehicle fuel tank, but also a number of containers in the boot of the vehicle.

By using ANPR technology on garage forecourts retailers are potentially able to provide conclusive video footage of offences to the police, On busy forecourts ANPR technology deployed with other forms of VCA software can also detect individuals who are filling additional fuel containers, before they have chance to drive away. Of course, over the last few years there has been a rapid increase in vehicle cloning. This is where criminals have altered, defaced or even totally replaced vehicle registration numbers in order to evade detection. However, sometimes the colour of the vehicle, together with any distinguishing marks on it such as dents or scratches, are sufficient to make a positive match with vehicles that have been entered onto a VCA database.

With such capabilities, the potential applications for VCA technology protecting retail premises, their staff and stock are endless. Unfortunately, as in most business cases, the application of VCA systems is quite often restricted by the cost involved in buying and installing them. This problem can be overcome by:

- **Shopping around** - Making best price comparisons between the manufacturers and suppliers of the products.

- **Price negotiation** - As is the case when most products are purchased, better deals can usually be struck dependant on the volumes involved and by comparing the prices offered by the competitors.

- **Considering the level of the technology required**- There are numerous systems available on the market, all doing different things. It is therefore important that the appropriate level of technology is being considered. It usually follows that the more functions a system can perform, the more it will cost.

- **Trials** - Try and negotiate a free trial of the proposed system with the manufacturers or suppliers. The results of such trials will have more clout with businesses Directors, than any amount of glossy sales brochures.

- **Cost/Benefit Analysis** - A thorough and realistic cost/benefit analysis should be completed that illustrates the potential benefits a system could provide for a business, such as greatly reduced unknown shrinkage figures. Purchasing such systems could then be considered as a form of long term investment for the business. The cost/benefit analysis would have even more credibility if it was based on an actual trial of the product.

CCTV monitoring

It matters not if the CCTV system that is installed on the business premises is the most expensive state of the art system that money can buy. It will be absolutely useless if no-one for or on behalf of the business takes any notice of it. If the primary reason for the installation of a CCTV system is purely to provide evidence in the event of a possible incident, then the cost and the scale of the system should be proportionate to these expectations. If this is not the reason that the system was installed then monitoring is required.

Internal Monitoring

Internal monitoring can range from being quite a simple to a fairly complex affair. In small businesses it is highly unlikely that there will be sufficient resources, either in the form of finances or personnel, to be able to permanently monitor CCTV equipment. In such instances careful consideration should be given to the positioning of monitors.

Provided that the positioning of monitors is not contrary to any of the provisions of the DPA 1998, they should be placed where the general staff can see them, such as near the tills. In addition it can also be beneficial to place monitors in such locations as the manager/admin offices, the cash office and even staff rooms. The more monitors that are available for viewing by all of the staff, the more likely it is that unknown shrinkage can be reduced.

In larger businesses, unless they have opted for external monitoring, it is common for them to monitor their CCTV systems internally, known as in house monitoring. If this is the case it is most likely that there will be a CCTV control room. The CCTV control room will normally contain:

- several monitors, the actual number of which will be dependent on the amount of CCTV cameras that need to be covered
- computer equipment or keypads for each CCTV operator

- DVRs, again numbers will be dependent on the size of the system
- cable racks
- secure cabinets for copy DVDs and other potential evidence
- radio equipment, telephone equipment
- CCTV operators.

Employed within the control room should be dedicated staff that have been properly trained to monitor CCTV systems. The CCTV operators should understand their role, be trained in what to look for *(never assume they already know)*, be trained in the completion and maintenance of CCTV control room documentation and procedures and have a full working knowledge of the requirements of the DPA1998. The number of staff required to carry out this function will also be dependent on the quantity of monitors and cameras that need to be managed. Unlike security guards, CCTV operators could find themselves directing personnel in the case of very serious incidents and their actions could be the difference between life and death. They will have to make decisions which security guards are not generally trained to do – they are trained to report to supervisors and await instructions – CCTV operators may not have the time for such luxuries. Training is essential!

If the staff is directly employed by the business, there is no legal requirement for them to be in possession of an appropriate Security Industry Authority (SIA) Licence. If the staff are employed by a third party supplier, such as a specialist Guarding Company, then they will require an appropriate SIA License.

External Monitoring

In cases where a business, small or large, wants the CCTV system to be monitored, but for whatever reason, do not want to do it themselves, they can hire the services of an external monitoring company to do it on their behalf. This kind of monitoring is usually carried out through an Internet Protocol (IP) connection, possibly from a control room hundreds of miles from the actual location of the cameras. Before such a Company is employed it is essential to ensure that they are an SIA approved Company and that they are registered with both the National Security Inspectorate (NSI) and the British Security Industry Association (BSIA). They should also have ISO 9001certification and provide evidence of sufficient insurance liability to cover all potential and likely eventualities.

Using a third party Company can be a cost effective way of monitoring CCTV systems, depending on how many systems are to be monitored. Monitoring companies normally base their charges on the following criteria:

- The number of cameras to be monitored.
- The types of cameras to be covered. (E.g. Fixed or Pan/Tilt/Zoom (PTZ)).
- The number of incidents they report.
- What action they are expected to take in the event of an incident being observed.
- Any other services that they may offer, such as attending the premises outside of normal working hours etc.

Irrespective of whether the monitoring of CCTV systems is internal or external, monitoring will most definitely assist with the detection of crime and help with reduction of unknown shrinkage.

CCTV Evidence

It is important to remember that where incidents have taken place and they have been recorded on a CCTV system, the recorded images may be required as evidence by the police to ultimately produce in a Court of Law, or by the business as evidence to support a case for disciplinary action. It is immaterial whether the CCTV evidence is to be produced in court or at a tribunal, it should be treated with exactly the same care. This means that regard should be given to both the security and continuity of the evidence (The full implications of what the term 'continuity of evidence' means is covered in a separate book in this series).

It is important that any CCTV images that show evidence of an incident or crime taking place are not altered in any way. This is particularly so when transferring the images from one means to another, such as from a computer hard drive on a disc. It is better to transfer too much footage than not enough, as this will negate any defence that presented footage was shown out of context and therefore did not truly represent the actual chain of events. The more important the evidence is, the more likely that the defence in a case will try and discredit it. If it is not possible to discredit the actual images, then attempts to discredit its evidential value may be directed at the means by which it was captured. It is therefore important that CCTV systems are regularly serviced and properly maintained.

Protection of equipment

The more efficient a CCTV system is at assisting with the apprehension of criminals, the more likely it is that attempts will be made to put it out of action. This does not only apply to systems that cover outdoor areas, but also to indoor areas. It should also be remembered that systems are just as likely to be tampered with by members of staff as they are by criminals entering premises with the sole intention of committing a crime. Almost every major crime committed against property in recent years has had the involvement of security personnel.

Some of the methods that are used to partially or completely disable CCTV systems and how they can be prevented are:-

- **Repositioning Cameras** - This can be quite a straightforward process, especially if they are internal cameras that are installed at a low level. It can be done by staff and criminals. Such tampering can be prevented by mounting the cameras in a higher position and if this is not possible, by mounting them in a security housing that will prevent them being moved. The same methods of prevention would also apply to external cameras. In addition, where cameras are mounted on poles, 'anti climb paint' can be applied to the top quarter of the poles, so that it will only effect anyone attempting to interfere with the cameras.

- **Covering/spraying camera lenses** - By quite simply placing a bag, cloth or anything similar over the camera lens, the camera is put out of action. The principle is no different to someone putting a blindfold on a human. This kind of issue can be prevented by once again mounting the cameras so that they cannot be reached, or by using ceiling mounted dome cameras.

- **Cutting through cables** - If there is no power source getting to a camera in order to operate it or work the telemetry, or the images that it is viewing are not being sent back to the monitor and recording device it is totally ineffective. This situation can be very easily achieved by quite simply cutting through the cables that are feeding into it. This can be avoided by making sure cables going into the back of a camera are routed well out of potential reach and where possible are not exposed. Where this is not possible they should be fitted inside armoured ducting. Furthermore, the use of wireless cameras can significantly reduce the amount of cabling required, significantly reducing the camera's vulnerability.

- **Isolating the power to monitors and recording devices** - This technique is usually one that is used by staff members at any level or corrupt security guards. It is a straightforward process of turning off the power feeding the equipment or switching the actual items of equipment off, using the switches on the equipment. To prevent this situation from occurring, all CCTV equipment should be wired directly into un-switched electrical spurs. These are basically plugs that do not have switches. They cannot be turned on or off as they are permanently on. Additionally, hard drives, DVRs and, for those that still operate them VCRs, should be locked in specially designed security cabinets.

- **Reprogramming systems** - Once again this is a technique that is usually carried out by staff members at all levels and corrupt security guards. It is basically a process of reprogramming the system so that it is not showing or recording images from a particular camera or cameras. The solution for this problem is to password protect the system so that how components operate can only be changed by an individual that holds the password. As a total failsafe the system should be placed inside a locked security cabinet to which access is very limited. System software should be secured in a fireproof safe only accessible by senior management.

- **Smashing recording equipment** – This speaks for itself and the only way to prevent or deter it is to make sure all cameras are in housing which is as secure as possible.

- **Tampering with recording devices** - This is becoming less common now as VCR's are replaced by other technologies. Tampering methods can include:-
    - Switching the recording mode off
    - Deliberately failing to set the system to record
    - Deliberately failing to change a tape cassette (VCR)
    - Deliberately changing a tape cassette so that it records over evidential footage (VCR)

- Ensuring that footage is being reviewed at the same time as an incident is taking place, so that images of the incident cannot be recorded.

Protection of Data

It is essential that all recorded data (images) is properly protected. This is for two main reasons; in order to comply with the DPA 1998, which is covered in detail in the next section, and just as importantly because the data may be required as evidence for internal disciplinary proceedings, and or Civil and Criminal prosecutions. Data protection does not just apply to unauthorised persons being able to take physical possession of the data but also includes unauthorised persons being able to view the data.

In general terms, data can be protected by ensuring that monitors are positioned so that they cannot be viewed by persons that are not entitled to view them. All forms of recording should be properly secured so that unauthorised persons are not able to download any of the images on to devices such as portable hard drives or data discs. It is important that the details of any downloads that are produced of CCTV images, from any part of the system, are recorded in a register. The records should be comprehensive, giving details of; when, by whom, for what purpose and whom they were given to. This is especially the case where images of individuals caught shoplifting are handed over to the police or are handed to representatives of the Personnel/HR departments.

CCTV Legislation

When CCTV systems were initially made available to both the general public and for business use there were no controls in place as to how they should be used without infringing a person's privacy. This situation is no longer the case as it is now legislated for in the UK by the Data Protection Act (DPA) 1998. Although this legislation applies to the UK only, other nations will probably have similar legislation. It is discussed here to provide guidance to loss prevention specialists on producing rules for the use of CCTV in any jurisdiction.

Data Protection Act 1998, (DPA 1998) – Relating to CCTV systems

As a result of the UK's requirement to act upon the European Directive on Data Protection, the Government formulated and passed the Data Protection Act 1998, (DPA 1998), to replace existing legislation. The DPA 1998 came into force on the 1st March 2000 and amongst the data that it applies too, it has also made specific provisions for data that is processed by CCTV systems.

Due to the ongoing advances in technology, most if not all CCTV systems, whether they are digital or analogue, will need to be compliant with the DPA 1998. The DPA 1998 not only creates legal obligations for organisations, but it also gives individuals rights, such as the right to gain access to their details and to claim compensation when they suffer damage. The extensions of rights for individuals and enhanced powers of the Information Commissioner, who polices the Act, means that compliance of the DPA 1998 and its Principles are of the utmost importance. There are potentially severe penalties against organisations that do not comply with this legislation.

As a result of the DPA 1998, the Information Commissioners Office (ICO) compiled a Code of Practice that provides recommendations for ensuring compliance with the legal requirements under the Act. The original draft Code of Practice was published in 2000 but was revised in 2008. The recommendations within the Code are all based on the legally enforceable Data Protection Principles that form the core of the DPA 1998 and have been set out to follow the lifecycle and practical operation of CCTV systems.

It is recommended by the Information Commissioner that all CCTV operators should comply with these Codes of Practice. The complete version of the DPA 1998 and the Information Commissioners Codes of Practice (revised) 2008 can be viewed on the internet (http://www.ico.gov.uk/). Let's examine some of the key points and the implications that the legislation has in relation to loss prevention and risk management.

In order to determine whether a CCTV system falls within the scope of the DPA 1998 detailed guidelines can be found within section 4 of the Act. It will be seen from these guidelines that it is most likely that the CCTV systems that are generally in operation in businesses today would fall within the scope of the Act. There are three main tests that should be considered when determining whether a CCTV system should comply with the Act, they are;

Is Data being collected? – Data is information which is;

> (a) Processed by equipment operating automatically in response to instructions given for that purpose.
>
> (b) Recorded with the intention that it should be processed by such equipment; or
>
> (c) Is recorded as part of a relevant filing system with the intention that it should form part of the relevant filing system.

It is important to note that the way data is processed is not limited to information processed by a computer, but includes any equipment that responds to instructions, such as images recorded on analogue video tape, or discs and via the medium of a camera. As video is no different from conventional methods of recording or storing data on magnetic media or computers, it means that all CCTV systems that record images by whatever means will be regarded as collecting Data.

It should also be noted that the DPA 1998 does not just relate to data produced or maintained on equipment. It also includes manual filing systems and these would include any reports, statements or other documents produced in a CCTV control room.

Is the Data being collected of a personal nature? – Personal Data is defined under the Act as data which relates to a living individual who can be identified from;

- The Data; or
- From that Data and other information that is in the possession of, or is likely to come into the possession of a surveillance team.

Some examples of activities that would result in the gathering of data of a personal nature in the loss prevention and risk management industry would be:

Where still photographs of known shoplifters are displayed on a notice board in a CCTV control room, or are kept in a manual filing system. It matters not whether names can be attached to the subjects of the photographs at that stage, the photographs are still identifying the person shown on them and are covered by the Act.

Monitoring staff behaviour and activities would constitute an act of collecting personal data because the staff would be known by their employers.

If a CCTV system accidentally records images of unknown people in a location where an incident has occurred, even if the perpetrator of the incident cannot be identified but passers-by or witnesses can, then the system will be classed as recording personal data, even though there is no interest in anyone other than the perpetrator.

Is the Data Automatically Processed by Reference to the Individual? – Within the Act there is no precise definition of what constitutes an act of 'processing' but it is generally interpreted as meaning any activity in relation to CCTV images, such as recording, displaying, printing, storing and destroying.

If any of the activities that have just been mentioned are taking place then the system will need to comply with the DPA 1998. This being the case the first step will be to register the business or organisation (formally known as notification) with the Information Commissioner. Failure to register is a criminal offence. Registration can be completed in the most part on the internet by visiting www.ico.org.uk but most businesses are likely to be registered anyway in connection with other business activities.

Once the system has been 'formally notified' then it must be operated in compliance with the eight Principles of the DPA 1998. It is beyond the scope of this book to go into these Principles in detail. Readers wishing to do so can find them on the ICO website, www.ico.org.uk . It is important to understand, however, that failure to comply with the principles could lead to very costly litigation claims which could seriously reduce an organisation's profit or working capital. For this reason the 8 Principles are included below.

Whether data is being gathered by CCTV or any other means it is important to remember the overriding principle of all UK Data Protection legislation:

- **Data must only be gathered for the purpose for which it was authorised and intended and must not be retained for any longer than is necessary.**

The Eight DPA 1998 Principles Relating To CCTV Are:-

1. Images will be obtained and used fairly and lawfully and CCTV systems will not be used unless:

> (a) The person subjected to monitoring gives their consent to do so; or
>
> (b) Monitoring is necessary for one of a number of specified purposes, including where necessary, for the purposes of legitimate interests of the user. (Except where the monitoring is unwarranted in any particular case, by reason of prejudice to the rights and freedoms and legitimate interests of the Data Subjects)
>
> (c) Where overt or covert surveillance is carried out for the purpose of:

(i) Crime prevention

(ii) Crime detection; or

(iii) The apprehension or prosecution of offenders

It will not be necessary for the operators to obtain the consent of individuals or to show that monitoring is necessary for the legitimate business interests of the user. The information Commissioner has confirmed that in 'limited and exceptional cases' use of covert cameras may be justified where the cameras are being used in an attempt to put a stop to 'specific criminal activity' involving 'specific individuals'. When monitoring is used for other reasons such as for Health & Safety purposes or monitoring employee performance, then the consent of the individuals being monitored would be required.

2. Personal data will be obtained only for one or more specified and lawful purposes, and will not be further processed in any manner incompatible with that purpose or those purposes.

To comply with this Principle access to images by third parties should only be allowed in limited and prescribed circumstances. If the purpose of the system is for the prevention and detection of crime, then disclosure to third parties should be limited to:

(a) Law enforcement agencies, such as the police, HMCE, etc. provided that the image is recorded to assist with a specific criminal investigation.

(b) Prosecution agencies such as the CPS or Health and Safety Executive.

(c) Legal representatives.

(d) The media when it has been assessed by the police that the public can assist in the identification of a victim, witness or perpetrator, in relation to a criminal incident. Under no circumstances should such images be passed to television production teams for the purpose of entertainment.

(e) The individuals whose images have been recorded and retained. This category however, would not apply if such disclosure would prejudice criminal investigations or criminal proceedings.

3. The monitoring or surveillance must be adequate, relevant and not excessive in relation to the purpose or purposes for which they are being processed.

Some examples of how to apply this Principle include:

(a) Positioning cameras so that systems do not record more information than is necessary. If the cameras are installed to monitor a lorry park, they should not overlook private residencies.

(b) Making sure that the operating quality of the equipment is good enough to be used as evidence. It is therefore essential that all equipment is properly installed and regularly maintained. Poor grade images may be deemed inadmissible evidence in court.

4. Images must be accurate and where necessary, kept up to date.

This Principle is of particular relevance if the personal information obtained from the system is to be used as evidence in civil or criminal judicial proceedings. It follows that caution should be exercised when using digital enhancement and compression technology, as the use of such technology can be used as a foundation for a defence that the images have been altered or taken out of context, thereby not truly reflecting the sequence of events that they are supposed to portray. This can be a potential issue when the continuity of the evidence that it is trying to illustrate is subjected to challenge.

5. Images recorded for any purposes will not be kept for longer than is necessary for that purpose or those purposes.

In terms of what is deemed to be for no longer than is necessary, the Information Commissioner's recommendations are that stills should only be taken from recordings when evidence is, or may be required of a specific activity and used in cases such as the detection and prosecution of offenders, or for internal disciplinary proceedings against employees.

In addition, tapes or digital storage mechanisms that have recorded the relevant activity should be retained until such times as proceedings are completed and the possibilities of an appeal have been exhausted. Where images are stored or recorded for circumstances other than these, the images should not be retained for any 'undue length of time'.

Within the DPA 1998 there is no definition as to what amounts to an 'undue length of time', instead the Information Commissioner has allowed individual businesses to formulate their own policy in this respect, based on the nature of the information and the purposes for which it is being collected. When formulating such policies it should be considered that it is a common occurrence that CCTV recordings that appear to be innocuous at the time they were created, can be of vital importance at a later point in time.

6. Personal data will be processed in accordance with the rights of data subjects under this Act.

Individuals are entitled to be informed about the reason for the monitoring and the location where the monitoring is taking place. Some of the reasons that are usually given to individuals regarding the necessity to monitor are for the purposes of:

    (a) Crime prevention

    (b) Crime detection

    (c) The apprehension or prosecution of offenders

(d) Personal safety

In order to comply with this Principle appropriate signs should be placed in and around areas where cameras are to be located. These signs should include such information as:-

(a) The existence of the cameras.

(b) The reasons for the monitoring.

(c) Who is conducting the monitoring?

(e) How the people conducting the monitoring can be contacted.

The purpose of the signage is to give individuals the opportunity to consent to being the subjects of surveillance and consent is assumed if the individual is still happy to proceed into an area where they know that they are being monitored. It is therefore necessary to display signage on the front of the premises or areas subject to surveillance, before an individual's image is captured by the cameras, thus giving individuals the choice to be monitored or not be monitored.

There has been a lot of discussion about the size of the signage, this is possibly owing to the fact that the precise dimensions are not legislated for. The signs need to be large enough to be prominent and easily noticed and the wording must be of a size that can be easily read by those that the notice applies to.

There is an exception to this Principle. The exception applies when individuals are the subject of covert monitoring, in which case their rights outlined in this Principle will not apply; that is of course provided, as previously stated in this section, that the covert cameras are being used in an attempt to put a stop to a 'specific criminal activity' involving 'specific individuals'.

Where camera systems for non covert purposes are being used then individuals' rights will apply. It is important that these rights are respected, not only in order to comply with the DPA 1998, but also in the interests of employer/employee relationships and significantly, the Human Rights Act 2000.

7. Appropriate technical and organisational measures will be taken against unauthorised or unlawful use of images and against accidental loss or destruction of or damage to, information arising from those images.

The word 'appropriate' could be interpreted in different ways by different individuals. Common sense would dictate that the more sensitive the images the more robust the security measures should be to protect them.

The considerations for such security should include:

(a) **The locations in which the cameras are located**:

(i) If the purpose of the CCTV system is the prevention and detection of crime, the cameras should be sited so that facial images are captured.

(ii) The cameras should be mounted so that they cannot be readily repositioned by person(s) not authorised to do so, or have their lenses in any way interfered with.

(b) **The physical security requirements of the security control room.**

(i) The security control room should be located in a part of the building that is separate to the operating functions of the business.

(ii) It should preferably have no windows, but if there are, all windows should be fitted with reinforced /obscure glass and further protected with security bars. If internal windows can be seen through they should be fitted with reflective film covering.

(iii) The entrance door should be in good working condition and be able to withstand any substantial attempts to force it open.

(iv) The entrance door should, at the very least, be fitted with good quality mortice locks, but preferably with an electronic access control system that is able to record the comings and goings of those that have entered the room.

(v) CCTV cameras that cover the operating equipment should be fitted inside the room

(c) **The monitoring of access to the security control room**.

(i) Access to the security control room should be restricted to designated or named members of staff and only these when they are on duty.

(ii) All operators should sign in at the beginning of their shift and sign out at the end. If operators leave the control room for any reason during their shift they should sign out and sign in again on each occasion.

(iii) Visitors should only be allowed access to the security control room if it is absolutely necessary and should be signed in/out and escorted at all times by a manager or designated member of staff.

(d) **The appropriate recruitment and selection of security control room staff**. It should be remembered that not everyone has the patience required to watch and analyse sometimes many monitors at a time. The task should therefore only be undertaken by those that want to do it and appear to have the aptitude to do it. It should also be remembered that;

(i) If the security control room is to be staffed by a third party Company then they will need to be in possession of a valid SIA licence.

(ii) Where internal security staff are chosen to operate the security control room, under current security legislation they do not need an SIA licence. They will not have undergone the vetting process that is part of the SIA licensing process but should be vetted to the requirements of British Standard 7858.

(e) **Ongoing training in Data Protection and Privacy issues.**

(i) All operators and employees with access to images should be aware of the procedures that need to be followed when accessing recoded images.

(ii) Training updates that are documented in the operators' training records are advisable in order to prove to the Information Commissioners Office that this has been carried out.

The training to be provided should include;

- An explanation of the security policy – the do's and don'ts for those that have access to recorded images.
- The disclosure policy to subjects of image recording.
- The rights of individuals in relation to their recorded images.

(f) **Control and monitoring of access to recorded material.**

(i) Access to recorded images should be restricted to a manager or designated member of staff, who will decide whether or not to allow requests for access by third parties in accordance with the documented disclosure policies.

(ii) Viewing of the recorded images should take place in a restricted area such as the security room manager's office.

(g) **The physical security of all recorded material.**

(i) Any CCTV recording must be held securely. In the case of analogue recordings on VHS tape this will mean a secure cupboard, locked unless access is required at a particular time, in which video cassettes will be held. Digital recordings will remain on the hard drive of the DVR for the proscribed time. Any copies from the DVR recording will be made onto DVD discs and these must also be kept securely, in a locked safe preferably.

(ii) Copies may have to be provided for a number of agencies; police, revenue and customs officials, solicitors, court and so on. Any copy leaving the control room must be signed for by an authorised person and details of the copy entered into a register maintained for the purpose.

(iii) Special security considerations should be given where images are transmitted to remote CCTV monitoring Stations

8. Personal data will not be transferred to a country or territory outside the European Economic Area unless that country or territory ensures an adequate level of protection for the rights and freedoms of data subjects in relation to the processing of personal data.

The Use of Covert Monitoring Systems

Firstly what do we mean by covert monitoring? It is the process whereby video or other recording equipment is used to monitor a person or persons without them being aware that the monitoring is taking place. The use of covert monitoring equipment against members of staff can sometimes be a rather drastic measure to take when trying to detect criminal activity in the workplace. Employers are subject to a duty of trust and confidence in respect of their employees, and vice versa. If covert surveillance systems are installed in the workplace, it is therefore possible that an employee could pursue a claim of breach of that duty, which would then be a matter for the Courts to consider in accordance with any Human Rights legislation. To pre-empt such problems it is always good practice to seek the agreement of employees regarding the business' surveillance policies, both overt and covert, through a consultative process. Such a process should be completed and the outcomes of the policy agreed prior to the installation of any system.

Even when surveillance policies have been agreed with the workforce, due to the potential detrimental effects on a business when using covert CCTV systems to monitor staff activities, the following should be considered when deciding whether or not to use covert monitoring systems in the workplace:

> (a) That covert surveillance, such as CCTV, should be used only in exceptional circumstances. A good indication of exceptional circumstances for the use of covert CCTV for instance, would be that there is good reason to suspect that criminal activity or similar serious malpractice is taking place and that the crime could not be detected by any other means.
>
> (b) That covert monitoring should only be used as part of a specific investigation. A covert CCTV system should not be installed to monitor workers on 'fishing trips'.

(c) That any covert CCTV cameras that are installed for a specific investigation should be removed as soon as the investigation is complete. Long term covert surveillance is not permitted under the terms of the DPA 1998 or under most Human Rights legislation.

(d) Has the decision to install covert monitoring systems been approved by the senior management? If not will they approve the use of them?

(e) Would it prejudice the outcome of the investigation to tell the workers that cameras are being used?

(f) Has the intrusion of innocent workers been taken into account?

(g) Will any images used in disciplinary proceedings be retained so that the person whose image it is can see it and respond?

(h) Has a written code of practice been prepared to deal with the covert system?

Covert monitoring equipment should never be installed in private areas such as toilets and private offices except in the most exceptional circumstances where a serious crime is suspected and will almost certainly result in the involvement of the police. It would not be acceptable to conduct this type of surveillance purely to provide evidence for an internal disciplinary matter.

It should be borne in mind that it is quite often the case that although a CCTV camera system is installed as an aide to a specific investigation, involving a specific suspect, it may produce evidence of other criminal behaviour conducted by someone that was not subject to suspicion. If this occurs this evidence should only be pursued if the offence committed is serious and amounts to a possible act of gross misconduct or misconduct that would put that individual or others at risk. The additional evidence should not be used for minor disciplinary matters.

Any use of CCTV should be properly documented at all stages, especially where covert systems are in place. Unless that documentation is properly maintained there is more than an even chance that evidence obtained using the system will be challenged and deemed inadmissible in legal proceedings, criminal or civil. In addition to potentially losing a criminal prosecution or employment tribunal case because the correct procedures were not followed, it should also be remembered that section 13(2) of the DPA 1998 entitles an individual to compensation for any unwarranted substantial distress or damages he or she suffers, due to the processing of personal data to which he or she is subject.

Chapter 4

Alarm Systems

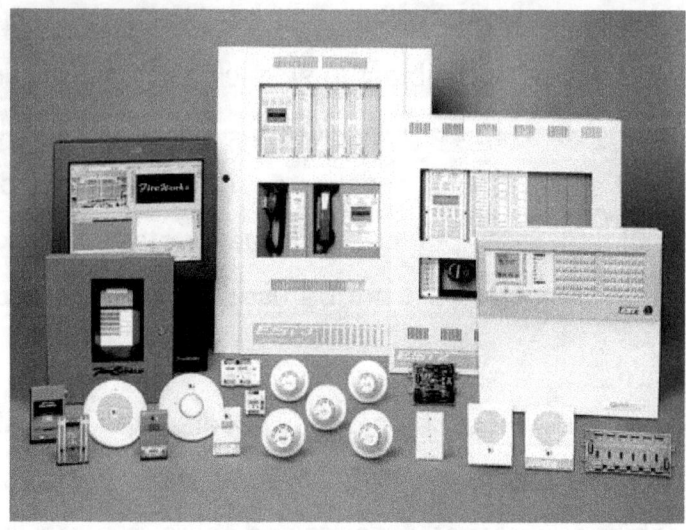

This chapter is dedicated to examining some of the alarm systems which are used to protect buildings, people, stock and other assets.

Intruder Alarm Systems

Intruder alarm systems or burglar alarms are perhaps the oldest group of electronic property protection devices that are still used today. They are basically designed to alert someone, usually by an electronic bell or siren, that there is an intruder in a restricted area.

How alarm systems work is of no consequence to a loss prevention specialist. The people who need to know how the systems work are those who supply, install and maintain them. You do, however, need a working knowledge of the different equipment used to make up an alarm system as you will doubtless be responsible for sourcing it, identifying the right equipment for your premises and negotiating cost and maintenance contracts.

What follows is a basic list of possible equipment which you might consider using in your alarm system:

Detectors

Passive Infrared Detectors (PIRs) - It is fair to say that of all the detectors that are used as part of an Intruder alarm system PIRs are the most common. This is so whether the intruder alarm system is operating on domestic or business premises. PIRs are relatively inexpensive to purchase and over the years have established a reputation for reliability. They can cover reasonably large areas and work by detecting changes in ambient infrared temperature.

Ultrasonic Detectors - Ultrasonic Detectors are rarely installed in new systems now but can be found in some older systems. They are motion detectors.

Microwave Detectors - The way a microwave detector functions is not too dissimilar to the way an ultrasonic detector works in that it is also a motion detector. They are more often found outside premises rather than inside.

Photo-Electric Beams - Photo-electric-beams operate by transmitting visible infrared light beams across the path of forced walkways or across doors and windows. These detectors are particularly effective because they can be used both internally and externally as a long range detection system, such as across a series of warehouse shutters or around the external perimeters of a building. They are activated when the light beam is broken.

Glass Break Detectors - This detector is ideal for use where there is a possibility that intruders could enter a building via a window. Glass break detectors are acoustic and vibration detectors designed to react to the specific noise and shock wave frequency that is produced when glass is broken. When glass is broken an alarm is activated.

Vibration Detectors (Vipers) - Vibration detectors are detectors that are usually mounted internally, against walls, where there is a possibility that intruders may try to break through in order to gain access. This is quite often the case when burglars are targeting safes or Automatic Teller Machines (ATMS). This detection relies on an unstable configuration in the electrical circuit. When movement or vibration takes place the unstable part of the circuit breaks, stopping the low current that flows around it, which in turn activates the detector.

The next group of detectors that we are going to take a look at are specifically for external use.

Passive Magnetic Field Detection - This is a fairly unusual type of technology in that it is normally buried in the ground to protect the approach to a protected area. It can also be used along the tops of walls to provide protection from intruders who gain access in that way. It works through an electromagnetic field (EMF) generator powered by two wires that are installed approximately 5" apart if used on a wall and 12" deep when used below ground. Activation is caused when a sensor detects a change in the magnetic field caused by someone, or something walking over it. If installed and configured correctly, this detection method is very reliable and is not prone to false alarms. Incorrect installation or configuration can lead to activation by wildlife so consideration must be given to the local geography before using this technology. Careful consideration should also be given as to where it is going to be installed as it will not function near high voltage cables or where radar is in use, such as near airports and some military bases.

H- Field - This is another detection system that relies on the disturbance of EMF. The system transmitter emits a radio frequency (RF) signal along a cable and then receives the signal back via another cable. It is activated if there is a difference in the signal that is received back, from the one that was originally transmitted, as this will have been caused by the introduction of an object, such as an intruder. It is important that the sensitivity is correctly set to avoid small animals and birds accidentally activating the system.

E- Field – Yet another detection system based upon the generation of EMF but in addition to being used on fences and walls it can also be installed on building perimeters. As an added bonus it can even be installed as a free standing detection system, on poles. Cables are connected to a signal processor that analyses the size of the intruder, movement of an intruder and how long the movement is taking place for. When all three aspects are detected at the same time the system activates the alarm. Unfortunately this detection system is prone to false alarms as it cannot distinguish between human and animal intruders, so cats and urban fox's will activate the system and even extreme weather conditions have been known to affect it.

Microwave barriers - Microwave barriers operate by transmitting an electromagnetic beam, which forms a sensitive but invisible wall of protection. The fact that it is invisible means that there is no way that an intruder will know where it is located. These walls of protection or barriers can therefore be used to protect the approach to buildings etc. Activation of the detector is initiated when a receiver detects that there are differences occurring within the beam that is producing the barrier. It analyses the differences and if it considers that they have been caused by an intruder the system is activated. The major issues with this type of detector is its vulnerability to false alarms. It is not the best choice of detector.

Micro-Phonic Detection - This technology is used to protect against attacks to chain link fencing, such as intruders climbing over them or cutting through them in order to gain access to the premises that the fences are protecting. The actual detectors for the system are usually attached to the fencing in the form of sensor cables, which transmit signals for analysis by the system. These signals are produced as a result of noise or vibration being generated.

Taut Wire Fence Systems – This method of detection for chain link fences is perhaps one of the most reliable types of technology available at present. Taut wire systems function by detecting movement at either end of wire sensors. Once again, this is a system which allows sensitivity of the detectors to be adjusted in order to prevent detection of minor movements caused by small animals or weather. Although this detection system is fairly old technology, it is still surprisingly expensive to purchase and install.

Fibre Optic Cables - This technology is based on the fact that fibre optic cables are very sensitive to disturbance. The system works by detecting differences in light emissions from the fibre optic cables.

Alarm Panels

Alarms are used in many functions around a business to warn of unwanted or dangerous activities. Intruders and fire are the two most common. Any alarm activation is the result of the detection of an unusual occurrence by the sensors discussed above. Signals are sent from the sensors to, normally, an alarm panel which analyses the signal and, if necessary, activates the alarm. Alarm panels come in various shapes and sizes depending upon their desired function.

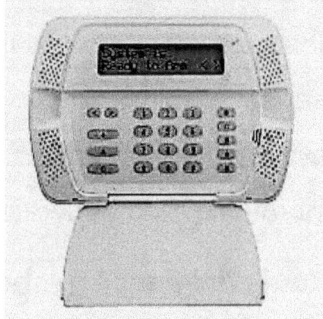

The arming, disarming, operating functions, monitoring functions and signalling functions of an intruder alarm system are all carried out using a control panel. Alarm panels can only be programmed, reprogrammed, armed and disarmed by individuals that are authorised to carry out these functions. Such authorisation is ultimately obtained from the alarm panel by entering codes into integral or separate but connected keypads, sometimes located near the point of exit/entry to the premises and or by use of traditional or electronic keys. In addition some of the latest systems available incorporate biometric technology to scan for fingerprints etc.

In order to ensure that only authorised people can enter the instructions into the intruder alarm panel there will normally be a hierarchy for codes. Some individuals will only be able to set or un-set the alarm with their codes. Others such as the manager, with the 'managers code', will be able to remove or install codes into the panel for new starters and leavers and the engineers with their codes will be able to service or re-configure it. Systems can also be programmed so that a separate duress code can be entered into the system that will unset the alarm as normal, but will alert those monitoring the system that there is a robbery or burglary taking place.

The failed authorisation, or the entry of a wrong code normally results in an alarm being immediately activated. Most alarm systems that are installed in businesses can be configured so that individual detectors or groups of detectors can be set or un-set separately in zones. This is a particularly useful function for large premises where some members of staff operate in only part of it at certain times. An example of this would be in a 24hr warehouse situation. The administration offices could be locked and alarmed during the night shift.

In terms of what an alarm panel can do, the list is almost endless. Their functions can include:

- The monitoring of both intruder and fire alarm systems on the same panel via separate channels,

- Enabling separate zones for each detector,
- Providing additional warning indicators such as mains loss, low battery warning, faulty detectors and/or damaged wires.

For additional functions this will depend on such factors as;

The type of alarm panel selected - Different alarm panels, made by different manufacturers, generally provide the same basic functions but can greatly differ in respect of the additional functions that they can be programmed to do.

What it will be expected to do - Clearly there is no point in installing a state of the art, multi zone, multi-function alarm panel costing thousands of pounds when it will only be connected to two PIR detectors.

Cost - As with most things in life, how much you are prepared to pay for an alarm panel will depend on the number of functions that it can be programmed to do.

New types of alarm panels are introduced frequently, the manufacturers of which freely boast about all the different things that their product can do. If, however, the panel is to be used for professional monitoring purposes, with expectations of police response in the event of an activation, then it will need to comply with standards and regulations governing installation and use. These will differ from jurisdiction to jurisdiction but some of these regulations and standards are covered at the end of this section.

Local (Bells Only) Systems

If an intruder alarm system is not being monitored, that is to say it is not linked in some way to a central point, where those responsible for monitoring such systems would follow an agreed course of action, it would be classed as a local or bells only system. With a 'bells only' system, if the detectors are triggered the externally mounted audible/visual warning, usually a bell or siren, will sound and strobe lights may flash. Depending on how old the system is the duration of the audible warning may range from 15 minutes (latest legislation for new installations) or until someone turns the system off.

The idea of operating the intruder alarm system in this way is the hope that it will alert someone living nearby or passing the premises, that something is wrong, in the belief that they will then contact the police. If there is an intruder, upon hearing the audible warning they will hopefully quickly vacate the premises. Unfortunately in reality, no one takes any notice of them, including the police. For this reason these alarms are usually fitted to domestic and not business premises.

Monitored Systems

Intruder alarm systems that are monitored for activations, commonly referred to as 'police response systems' are generally found to be in operation in most businesses. Contrary to popular belief, intruder alarm activations are not signalled directly to the police, unless the signal is from a system that they have installed in relation to a specific operation.

In normal circumstances when there is an alarm activation involving a monitored system, the external audio/visual alarm will usually still sound/show, unless a 'silent 'system is being used. In addition, the activation signal will also be sent by various methods, some of which we are about to cover, to an Alarm Receiving Centre or ARC. Depending on what services have been agreed with the ARC, they will respond to the situation.

Services that an ARC can provide have increased dramatically over recent years. In addition to informing key-holders that there has been an Intruder alarm activation and, where appropriate, informing the police of the situation in order that they can attend the premises, they also monitor;

- Access control systems
- CCTV Systems
- Fire alarm systems
- Sprinkler systems
- Critical Conditions
- personal attack alarms (PAB's)

- Open and Close signals (Setting/Un-setting of alarm systems)
- Duress signals
- The Communication method from the intruder alarm system to the ARC for tampering

In addition to these services they are also able to, via secure internet log on, provide reports and exception reports relating to the systems that they are monitoring.

Some of the different communication methods by which an ARC may receive Intruder alarm activation signals are:

- A standard telephone line – Dial up Network
- A digital dialler (Digi Dialler)
- A tamper resistant Fibre Optic Cable
- A specially encoded Mobile Telephone
- An standard Internet Interface
- IP messages via Broadband

Once the ARC has received an Intruder alarm activation signal from premises that it is monitoring, what it does with this information will depend on a number of factors; the alarm zone that has been triggered, the number and sequence of alarm zones that have been triggered and the time of day or night that it was triggered. Once these factors have been considered the

ARC will then initiate an appropriate course of action which could include:

- Contacting the police and requesting that they attend the premises. Provided that the alarm system for the premises is registered with the police for attendance.

- Contacting the key-holders of the premises and request that they attend the premises.

- Contacting a designated key-holding company authorised to attend the premises on behalf of the premises owners.

- Inform a designated guarding company to attend the premises on behalf of the premises owners.

Some intruder alarm systems are also integrated with the premises CCTV systems, which enable staff from the ARC to look into the site to establish if the alarm activation is a genuine one, i.e. an intruder can be seen on the premises or not. If an intruder can be seen on the premises this information is usually passed to the police, together with the actual whereabouts of the intruder. The recorded footage of the incident may at a later date be recovered by the police for evidential purposes.

In some circumstances instead of using CCTV systems to verify that intruder alarm activations are genuine, some of the ARC's business clients have installed 'Listen In' intruder alarm monitoring systems. These are systems where speakers and microphones have been installed on the monitored premises, allowing the ARC staff to firstly listen for noises that would indicate that there are intruders on the premises and then potentially speak to them, possibly to warn them that they have been discovered and that the police are on their way. This of technology is particularly useful when monitoring lone workers, such as security guards that may be working on business premises.

Intruder Alarm Surveys

Before rushing in and installing the first intruder alarm system that an intruder alarm company is trying to sell you, a comprehensive survey should be conducted in order to establish:

- **The areas to be protected** - internal/external areas, all of the premises, some of the premises etc.

- **The type(s) of detectors required** - movement detectors, vibration detectors etc.

- **The type(s) of intruder alarm technologies required** – Perimeter fence protection

- **The type of signalling** - If the intruder alarm system is to be monitored then it will need to be capable of sequential signalling. This is when two or more detectors sequentially detect a condition that they are each supposed to detect, trigger the alarm. In an attempt to reduce the number of false alarms it is no longer possible for just one detector to activate the system.

- **The type(s) of alarm panel required** – any alarm panels chosen will need to be compatible with the detectors and technologies that are selected. Most important of all, they will need to be reliable.

- **Will the intruder alarm system be monitored?** - If the answer to this question is yes, then during the survey consideration will need to be given to the requirements of, in the UK, the Association of Chief Police Officers (ACPO) policy and compliant to such installation standards as PD662:2004 and DD243.

- **The budget** – What would ideally like to be installed may be restricted by what can be afforded.

- **Who will monitor the system?** - If it is to be monitored what services will the monitoring company be expected to provide?

- **Who will install and maintain the system?** - Ideally one company should be responsible for both functions in order to ensure the validity of the manufacturers and installers guarantees.

When it comes to conducting the actual intruder alarm survey, consideration should be given to the integration of a number of security methodologies and not just those relating to intruder alarms. The methodical approach to effective security is to detect, delay, and to alarm.

It would therefore follow that it may sound like a good idea to install detectors of some kind on the perimeter fence of the premises, in order to detect and delay the intruder, but before this can be done there will need to be a fence to begin with. If there is already a fence, it will need to be in good order. If there is no fence then the delay methods will be on the premises themselves, such as strong doors and windows, fitted with good quality locks. Should the intruders get past these then they will be detected by the intruder alarm, which will then alert someone about the intrusion. Although this may sound obvious, these things are not always considered in a methodical way and logic often gives way to over exuberance when faced with a salesperson trying to sell his or her latest hi-tech 'toy'.

Detailed drawings, equipment specifications, and the details of proposed maintenance contracts should be attached to a cost benefit analysis when a request for expenditure for the installation of an intruder alarm system is submitted for approval.

Intruder Alarm Regulations

Intruder alarm systems have their own regulations that will need to be adhered to. For monitored systems the regulations are formulated by ACPO. During this section we will look at what complying with these regulations will entail.

ACPO Policy

Having made the decision to install an intruder alarm system on business premises it is then important to decide if the system to be installed is to be a 'Monitored System' (Type A) or 'Bells Only (Type B). The former is usually installed with a view to obtaining an immediate response from the police if the system or any part of it is activated and is commonly referred to as a police 'response' system.

It should be noted at this juncture that the decision as to whether a 'bells only' or 'police response' system should be installed is usually influenced by the insurance cover the business has in place. The majority of insurers do not permit the installation of a 'Bells Only' system for an unmanned, or partially unmanned site, and those that do, do so as a result of greatly inflated insurance premiums and/or on the understanding that additional or enhanced physical security measures that meet their satisfaction are implemented.

When it has been decided that a 'police response' system is to be installed, the chosen system, together with the installation and ongoing management of it, will need to comply with the ACPO policy, specifically the 'Security System Services Policy 2004' (Revised 2010). If a Type 'A' intruder alarm system does not comply with this ACPO policy at the time of installation or at a later time after the installation, then police Response will not be granted or will be withdrawn, and the police will not respond to any subsequent activations.

When first examining the ACPO policy it looks very complex and appears to have very little to do with the response of the police to an alarm activation, but more to do with the installation and actual workings of intruder alarm systems. In part this would be an accurate observation, however, in order to understand why this is the case it is important to understand the background of the documents compilation.

Until the beginning of the early 1970's the police invariably used to provide an immediate and almost rapid response to all intruder alarm activations. About this time three things changed that would eventually make such a vital service provided by the police both impractical and an unworkable burden, unless procedural changes were made. These were:

(1) The introduction of remote signalling alarms.

(2) The significant increase in the number of intruder alarm systems installed. This was brought about as a result of cheaper technology and increases in burglaries.

(3) The disproportionate rise in false alarms.

This state of affairs was not beneficial to anyone, for the police wasting time on false alarms and to the victims of genuine activations that the police did not have time to respond to as a result of dealing with other incidents and false alarms elsewhere.

As a result of this ever increasing problem ACPO compiled a formal policy aimed at reducing the number of false calls passed to police control rooms. The original policy has been updated a couple of times in order to introduce stricter limits on the number of acceptable false alarms and to also allow for changes in technology.

Before we look at the main points of the policy it should be borne in mind that Appendix A of the document is a provision for individual police forces that enable them to adapt or add additional requirements to the policy, relevant to their particular force area of responsibility. It is therefore important to be aware of any such amendments as they will need to be adhered too in order to qualify for police response to intruder alarm activations.

Main Points of the ACPO policy:

The ACPO Policy applies to all 'A' remote signalling systems terminating at recognised alarm Receiving Centres (ARC's) and Remote Video Response Centres (RVRC's). The ARC's and RVRC's must conform to BS 5979 (Cat II) in order that Unique Reference Numbers (URN's) can be issued by the police for their systems. Activations received from an ARC/RVRC without a current URN will be treated as a B system and will not receive a police response without evidence of an offence in progress.

The installation and services provided by the installing company and ARC will be certified by a UK Accreditation Service (UKAS) accredited certification body such as the National Security Inspectorate (NSI).

The police will respond to security system activations either as a result of a confirmed activation via an ARC, or where a person at the scene reports an offence in progress and requests police attendance. There are two levels of response:

> **(1) Level One – Immediate response (subject to priorities)**. To receive police response for a remotely monitored alarm system, any systems installed after 2005 must conform to PD662:2004 and DD243.

> **(2) Level Three – Response withdrawn**. This level occurs as a result of three false calls to the police relating to intruder alarms, or two relating to personal attack alarms (PAB's) in a twelve month rolling period. Reinstatement can be obtained once the cause of the false alarms has been identified and rectified.

(NB) There used to be a level two response defined as – 'desirable but not essential', but this level has now been abolished under the 2010 revision of the Policy.

Each police Force will maintain a list of alarm installation companies that conform to the ACPO Policy. Only companies on this list may install, maintain or monitor Type 'A' systems.

Premises with A systems will have at least two key-holders, the details of which will be maintained by the ARC/RVRC or via arrangements with a central key-holding company service. Key-holders will;

    (a) Be trained to operate the alarm.

    (b) Be contactable by telephone.

    (c) Have transport to attend the premises at all hours.

    (d) Be able to attend within 20mins of being notified to do so.

    (e) Have access to all relevant parts of the premises.

Failure of key-holders to attend when requested to do so on three occasions in a rolling twelve month period will result in the withdrawal of police response for a three month period.

The installer, maintenance company, ARC and customer have an obligation to employ all possible means to filter out false alarm calls to the police. For the benefit of the Policy a false alarm call is defined as a call that has been passed to the police but has not resulted from;

(a) A criminal attack, or attempts at such

(b) Actions by the emergency services in the execution of their duties.

(c) A call emanating from a personal attack/lone worker PAB

(d) Requests made by RVRC's for police to attend a sighting of individuals seen on protected premises where no criminal activity, attempt/intent is in progress, will be considered as civil trespass and such calls would be classified as false.

(e) Activation of detectors without apparent damage or entry to the premises and line faults will be considered as false alarms unless proved otherwise.

Following the withdrawal of police response it will only be reinstated if it is an unconfirmed system that is upgraded to a confirmed DD243 (2004) system.

PAB's may be operated to summon urgent police assistance when a person is threatened with immediate personal violence or a criminal act. It must not be used for any other reason. Misuse of PAB's may result in a level 3 response being imposed by the police.

Product Protection

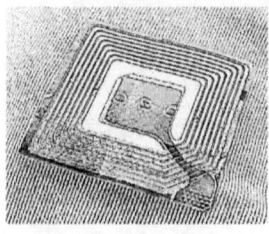

Over recent years use of alarm systems have become increasingly popular for the protection of stock. This is in part because there are a greater number of technologies to choose from and because of the efficient and mass produced electronics used. They have become more affordable.

General Types

A number of the systems that are in use work on the basic principle of a wire or cable passing through the product, normally clothing or DIY tools, and then into a control box forming an electrical circuit. If the wire or cable is cut, thus breaking the circuit, an audible alarm is activated. This type of system is generally referred to as a 'Loop alarm'.

It is not always possible to pass a wire or cable through a product, as is the case with electrical items such as mobile telephones, televisions and computers. In these cases the systems work by sticking contacts onto the product which, if removed before they have been isolated from the control box, will also result in an audio alarm being activated.

One of, if not the most common product protection methods that is used by retailers, is the use of security tags.

Electronic Article Surveillance (EAS) Systems

EAS systems originally used by retailers for the protection of stock were 'tagging' only. This is the process of attaching reusable plastic tags to the products. The tags are usually in the form of a coloured plastic disc, the colour being dependent on the radio frequency that it reacts to and the manufacturer of the tag. The disc is attached to the product by pushing a small metal pin through the product and into the disc. The tag can only be removed from the product by using a strong magnet that releases the pin from the disc. The alarm is triggered by the tag activating the electronics in pedestals located at the entrance and exits of the retail premises. The theory behind the use of these systems is that if the item has been paid for the tag would have been removed at the point of sale, thus preventing alarm activations.

Although 'tagging' in this form is still practised, the technology behind the systems has changed dramatically. Now reusable plastic tags, which could in the main only be attached to items of clothing, take the form of disposable labels, called RF (Radio Frequency) ID tags. These can be stuck to almost any product, both by the retailer and at source by the manufacturer of the product. Instead of being removed at the point of sale after the item has been paid for, these tags are quite simply deactivated.

The technologies used for the detection of the tags, depending on which is used, will be based on Radio Frequency (RF),

Acousto-magnetic (AM) and Electromagnetic (EM) technologies.

Radio Frequency (RF) - The tags that use RF technology look very similar to RFID labels. Built into the tag is a metal coil (inductor) and a capacitor which are wired in series. In order for the pedestal to detect the tag, it sends out a RF signal in a range of different frequencies to accommodate different tags. This causes the activated tags to resonate and then be detected by the pedestal. To deactivate the tag it is passed over the top of a high energy transmitter at the point of sale which blows a built-in fuse that partially destroys the capacitor.

Acousto- Magnetic (AM) - The workings of AM tags comprise two metal strips that are magnetised when the tag is activated. One of the pedestals (transmitter) located near the entrance/exit transmits a pulse which causes the metal to oscillate. The other pedestal (receiver) detects the tag when the transmitter is in between pulses, but a signal is still resonating from the tag. These tags are easily deactivated by demagnetising them at the point of sale.

Electromagnetic (EM) - Electromagnetic tags operate in exactly the opposite way to Acousto-Magnetic ones in that they are fitted with a single metal strip that is de-magnetised in order to activate them. The detection method in this particular case is by a low frequency current which is transmitted from the pedestal, causing the tag to generate a harmonic frequency that is picked up by the receiver signal processing. To deactivate the tag it will need to be magnetised at the point of sale.

Before deciding which type of technology to install in a retail business consideration should be given to the following issues:

Is there an EAS system already in operation in other areas of the business? – Unless the plan is to replace the complete EAS system that is being used by the business the same technology should be used when it comes to new installations.

Frequency range - The frequency range of transmitting and receiving pedestals should be the same for every location within the business. The reason for this is because the tags and labels are manufactured to operate at specific frequencies that cannot be altered on the tag by the retailer, unlike the pedestals where the frequency can be altered. Supplying and re-supplying tags becomes a nightmare for a business to manage if it has to purchase several different sorts of tags that function at several different frequencies not all compatible with all of the pedestals in operation.

What systems and transmitting frequencies are being operated by nearby retailers?- This is important to establish in order to prevent false activations of the pedestals being caused as a result of similar tags being used by the systems of nearby retailers. This is a common problem encountered in shopping centres and high streets where retail outlets operate in close proximity to each other.

What types of products are to be protected? - Depending on the types and quantities of products that need protecting will depend on the volumes and types of tags required. If the retail business is a clothes shop; then perhaps only the hard disc tags will be required, not the RFID .

The type of pedestals to be used - The pedestals come in all shapes and sizes and materials, depending on the manufacturer, the size of the premises, and the technology used. In some cases the EAS technology can even be fitted into door frames, which is ideal for small premises. Some retailers use the free standing pedestals to display point of sale advertising material that has been especially made to fit over or around the pedestal.

Costs - The cost of EAS technology can vary depending on the technology to be used. However, in addition to considering the outright purchase of EAS systems, most suppliers will also provide the systems on finance terms, thereby making it more affordable.

EAS management – One of the most important aspects of EAS management is staff training. It does not matter if the latest, most expensive EAS system on the planet has been installed, it will be absolutely worthless if the staff do not react appropriately when the system is activated. I am sure we have all experienced the situation when we have paid for an item but, when we attempt to leave the premises the alarm in the pedestals goes off. Apart from you standing there feeling guilty about nothing, no one else bothers to see what the problem is.

This situation more commonly occurs when label RFID are being used incorrectly. In situations where the tags are not being properly deactivated the staff will lose interest in the alarm sounding and will not bother to react to it anymore. Once this situation occurs, the system may as well be switched off as it will be useless as a deterrent to shoplifting.

This situation can sometimes happen with the disc tags as well, but the additional problem here is that when the customer gets the product home and discovers that there is still a tag attached to their item of clothing, they will not be able to get it off. They will then have to return it to the retail outlet in order for them to do so. This is not the way to impress customers and make them want to return to the store again.

Buying the re-useable tags and the pins used to attach them is quite an expensive one on an ongoing basis. It is common, however, to see them being unnecessarily thrown away by the staff. This practice must be stopped as quickly as possible as the replacement of the tags is a cause of unnecessary business shrinkage.

As previously mentioned the hard tags are supplied in different colours depending on the frequency they operate at, this is so that they cannot be mixed up. However, in situations where there are a number of outlets in the business and some of them are using different systems, it is possible for the tags to become mixed up. The staff must be trained to sort the tags out, removing any colours that they do not normally use, as it is highly unlikely that they will work with the system, making it a waste of time fitting the tags to the products in the first place.

EAS Vulnerabilities

As with most technologies there are ways for criminals to circumnavigate their way around most EAS systems. The most common method to render an EAS system useless is by using bags lined with kitchen tin foil to steal the items fitted with tags. The foil acts as a screen once the article has been placed in it, preventing the pedestals from picking up any of the signals from the tags.

Other methods of bypassing EAS systems used by the thieves include removing or deactivating the tags with the use of strong magnets or deactivating devices, which have sometimes been stolen from the retail outlet prior to stealing the merchandise. It is therefore important not to allow such items to get into the wrong hands. This can easily be achieved by ensuring that they are not left lying around and that they are properly mounted, or attached by security cables to the points of sale.

Where this continues to be a problem then consideration should be given to implementing non-EAS tagging as well, in the form of such things as non-freezable dye tags. They will need to be non-freezable as thieves have discovered if the merchandise is placed in a freezer the dye will freeze solid, allowing the tag to be broken off, without fear of the dye damaging the merchandise.

Finally where EAS systems are using the disc tags, care should be taken when fitting them to the merchandise so that they do not damage the item and that tags are fitted to every item, otherwise the thieves will only take the untagged items.

Additional Applications

In addition to the fundamental applications that an intruder alarm system is used for, there are some additional ones that can be used in conjunction with them. We will now take a look at one or two of them.

Secondary Internal monitoring

Although in circumstances where intruder alarms are monitored by third party companies, these companies will, upon request, provide exception reports. These are usually at additional expense and although with the latest technology the reports can be provided fairly quickly, it is advantageous for a business to be able to examine and analyse the data produced from the alarms itself.

Such analysis will provide information such as:

- **Are the intruder alarms being set at all?** – This is important to know prior to and after burglaries have been committed. If they are not disciplinary action should be considered against those responsible for setting the alarms.

- **The time they are being set** - This could provide an early indication that particular sites may be closing earlier than they are supposed to.

- **Unauthorised setting and un-setting** - This could provide an early indication that something is amiss at a site, such as the staff returning to the site for criminal purposes.

- **Key holder attendance for alarm activations** - This could provide an early indication that they are not attending the sites at all or not within the time parameters stipulated by ACPO. Such negligence could result in the suspension or withdrawal of police response arrangements.

- **As a quality control** - Having this facility is a good way to make sure that the third party monitoring company are providing a service that meets the standards and levels of service that have been agreed and are being paid for by the business.

Personal Attack Alarms (PAB's)

An additional function to a monitored intruder alarm system is that they can also function as a personal attack alarm, by having personal attack buttons (PAB's) connected to them. PAB's are normally connected to the system by a separate channel. Under ACPO policy, activations from these devices are treated separately to intruder activations and are duly allocated a separate 'false alarm' tolerance. It is possible to lose police response facilities for the intruder alarm, as a result of exceeding the number of permitted false alarm activations, but still retain police response facilities for the PAB's.

In order to reduce the number of false PAB activations, the devices that are installed, usually in cash offices, near the points of sale, in reception areas, or anywhere else where staff feel vulnerable to the threat of violence, normally comprise of a duel button system. Both buttons have to be pressed in order to activate the alarm. This reduces the possibility of an activation being initiated as a result of accidentally pressing one of the buttons.

Stand alone or remote PAB's can sometimes be used in addition to this, fixed and hard wired. . These are ideal for lone workers, or workers that operate in no specific location within the business and work when activated by a radio signal that is transmitted to the alarm panel. Some devices are also programmed to activate automatically if the wearer of the device should adopt a horizontal position, as in the case of a medical collapse or physical attack.

It is most important that when using these devices, when they are activated that UNDER NO CIRCUMSTANCES should they trigger an audible alarm at the site where they are operated. This can provoke further attacks by an assailant.

All members of staff that may be expected to use PAB's should be properly trained as to when and how to operate them.

CCTV interface

In situations where both intruder alarms and CCTV systems are installed at a site consideration should be given to interfacing the two systems as this can be achieved at very little extra cost. By doing this it will provide additional security functions such as:

- The CCTV cameras switching to cover doors and pathways where there have been intruder alarm activations.
- CCTV cameras switching to cover EAS pedestals that have been activated.
- CCTV cameras switching to areas where other electronic product protection devices have been activated.

- CCTV cameras switching to cover areas where there has been a PAB activation.

Footage of such activations can be an invaluable additional form of evidence to support all forms of criminal prosecutions.

Chapter 5

Personnel

One of the most important assets within any business is the personnel. How good the personnel are at their jobs will have a direct impact on how successful the business is. This statement is particularly true of the personnel that work within the divisions that make up the loss prevention and risk management departments. Depending on how good the staff are at doing their jobs within this part of a business will have a direct impact on known and unknown shrinkage levels.

It is therefore important when establishing an effective loss prevention and risk management department within a business, that the right quality of staff with the appropriate qualifications and experience are selected for each of the roles.

During this section we will examine the ways that a risk management and loss prevention function can be established within a business together with the advantages and disadvantages associated with the different approaches.

In-House Security Teams

One of the most common approaches to loss prevention and risk management is for a business to operate an 'in-house' security team. The term 'in-house' denotes that the staff is on the payroll of the business and as such they have a contract of employment with the business. Depending on the size of the business the security team could comprise of all, or a selection of the following roles:

- **Security guards** - These are generally uniformed staff that operate at office locations, distribution sites or in retail outlets such as supermarkets and shopping centres. The role of the 'in house' security guards is normally to physically protect the staff and customers. The subject of security guards is covered in more detail under the headings of External and Internal Manned Guarding later in this section.

- **Store Detectives** - Store detectives are usually dressed in plain clothes and operate covertly in retail outlets in order to identify and apprehend shoplifters. Store detectives must have a clear and comprehensive understanding of what constitutes an act of theft and what their powers of arrest are. Store detectives that are directly employed by the business, that is to say, 'in house' do not need to be licensed by the SIA.

- **Loss prevention personnel** - Loss prevention operators and loss prevention managers once again generally operate in plain clothes and are responsible for a group of retail outlets or businesses that are split into areas or regions. Usually a number of retail locations make a retail region. Irrespective of whether a loss prevention team is responsible for an area or a region, the responsibilities will be roughly the same; to protect the company's profit, assets and personnel.

- **Risk management managers** - Risk management managers are plain clothes operatives that are responsible for assessing all situations that are or could pose a threat to the business. Once such threats or potential threats have been identified it is the responsibility of the risk manager to provide recommendations as to how the threat can be totally eradicated or properly managed in the event that it should materialise.

- **Retail Audit staff** - retail audit staff can be an integral part of a security department, in that they are managed by the head of that department, or they can work to a separate department altogether, such as the finance department. The information they provide is essential in identifying both known and unknown stock shrinkage. It also assists in the provision of supporting evidence relating to misdemeanours, for use during internal disciplinary procedures, tribunals and civil and criminal court prosecutions.

- **Corporate Security Managers** - The main responsibilities of Corporate Security Managers are normally in relation to looking after Head Office locations and dealing with security matters directly related to corporate issues. They also usually instrumental in formulating Company security polices, major incident and disaster recovery plans.

- **Administrators** - A security department will always have need of administrators in order to:
    - Produce narrative reports
    - Compile statistical reports
    - Check Invoices

- Input Data

Personnel Selection

The appropriate selection of personnel for each of the above roles cannot be overstated. Although the difference in required skill sets and aptitudes for some of the roles may in some cases be apparent; such as those that would be required by an auditor or a loss prevention manager, some are not. This particularly applies to such roles as security guards.

Security guards are utilised in specific roles as was briefly mentioned above and it follows that there are also different aptitudes and skill set requirements for the different guarding roles. Security guards that have previously been employed at a busy distribution site may not be suitable reemployed in a supermarket environment, where there a long periods of inactivity, and *vice versa*. Likewise it does not always follow that a recently retired policeman with thirty years of service will always make a good loss prevention manager, especially if the person has no retail experience

It is therefore important that before a person is appointed for any of the above roles that they can produce evidence of previous appointments held, together with a proven track record relating to the roles for which they are seeking employment. In addition, further probing, in the form of extensive questioning and/or aptitude tests should take place prior to a job offer being made. On the subject of aptitude tests, many of those commercially available do nothing to establish the ability of a person to do the job for which they are being tested. Tests should be formulated to examine the ability of a person to do the tasks they would be expected to do. In the case of loss prevention personnel for example, can the person analyse a situation, decide what needs to be done and act upon those decisions? Similarly, can they communicate verbally and in writing? If not, they will not make very good loss prevention operators.

Training

When recruiting for a new appointment, the job should go to the person who is the best qualified and experienced to undertake the role to be filled. The subject of training should play an important part in the decision making process. It will need to be established what level of training the applicant has already undergone, and what level of training the applicant still needs to undergo if they are offered a position. No matter how suitable an applicant appears to be in terms of formal or informal training they say they have undertaken, or any qualifications they claim to hold, where appropriate documentary evidence should always be sought to substantiate such claims supplemented with in depth questioning.

Although it is always ideal to employ someone who is highly qualified it should be remembered that the more qualified a person is the greater their salary expectations will be. The less qualified they are the more money may need to be spent on them to train them to an appropriate standard. For financial reasons it is also important that an applicant is not over qualified for the role advertised, because their salary expectations, relative to their qualifications, if met, will be an unnecessary financial cost to the business.

Realistically, no matter how well qualified an individual is there will always be a certain amount of training that they will have to undergo in their new position, such as familiarisation of company policies and procedures.

Costs

Running a security team of any size, whether it comprises a loss prevention department run by one manager, or operates with only two security guards, it will be an expensive ongoing cost that will increase year on year. When deciding on the specific roles that need to be undertaken and the number of staff required to fill the roles it can easily be overlooked that in addition to budgeting for their salaries, there are additional costs to take into account such as:

- National Insurance Contributions
- Uniforms (where applicable)
- Cars; and all of the associated leasing, servicing and Insurance expenses

- Fuel
- Temporary cover for long term sickness
- Temporary cover for Maternity leave
- Training
- Payment of Company Bonuses
- Pension schemes (Contributory and Non Contributory)
- Share schemes
- Incremental Pay Rises
- Potential Overtime costs

Advantages

The main advantage of employing in house security teams is that because they are directly employed by the business and therefore directly controlled by the business, they are more likely to be an integral part of the business. If they are managed properly they will usually work towards the same aims, goals, targets and values of the business. If they do not, the business is in a position to deal with these members of staff in exactly the same way as any other member of staff that is on their payroll.

Disadvantages

Perhaps the major disadvantage for a business employing an 'in house' security team has to be the cost. However, if managed properly it should be possible to justify the costs of such services by producing evidence of what the services have saved the business, hopefully in terms of reduced unknown shrinkage figures.

Unfortunately the success of a security team can be the cause of its own demise and subsequent job losses. In reality it is only possible to reduce unknown shrinkage to a certain level, it will never be possible to totally eradicate it. Once this level has been attained and maintained for some time, it is a common misconception by the businesses Directors that the security team are not performing sufficiently and so either reduce the size of the team or get rid of it altogether. This can particularly be the case when a business is faced with financial hardship. However, reducing or getting rid of the security team altogether will ultimately compound any financial difficulties, as invariably the unknown shrinkage figures will once again start to rise.

Another disadvantage of operating an 'in house' security team is that it is a quite inflexible way of doing things when it comes to maintaining staffing levels. No business will be in a position to carry additional staff in order that they can cover for sickness and holidays etc. Any staffing shortfalls will have to be covered by overtime payments to the staff that are working. Depending on when the overtime is worked it will need to be paid at time and a half or double time rate. During the course of a year this can amount to quite an additional sum of cash to be found from someone's budget.

Another aspect of inflexibility that also relates to staffing levels is that unlike with staff supplied by third party companies, the 'in house' staffing levels are not as easy to adjust, especially at short notice. This can be a particular problem at peak operating times of the year, such as Christmas and sales periods, and even during certain times of the week.

A potential solution to counteract the disadvantages of operating with 'in house' security teams is to operate them in conjunction with some staff supplied by third party companies. If the sums add up, the loss prevention function could be completely replaced with services supplied by a third party Company.

Non-Dedicated Security Teams

In order to reduce costs more and more, businesses are operating without dedicated security teams and instead incorporating such roles within other roles conducted by other people within the business.

Selection

One of the most common methods of delegation of the security role is to make retail area and regional managers ultimately responsible for the day to day security of their designated outlets, supported by other areas of the business such as the property/estates/facilities and HR/personnel departments. The retail area/regional managers' roles would then include such matters as ensuring that loss prevention policy is being adhered to by their outlet managers and the investigation of security breaches. Matters relating to security equipment, such as intruder alarms, CCTV, EAS systems etc., would be managed by the property/estates/facilities department and the hiring of security guards and store detectives would be the responsibility of the HR/personnel department.

Training

If this is the chosen method of managing the security functions within a business, then there will be a requirement to properly train those individuals involved. After all they will not have been employed for possessing the required skill sets needed by security or loss prevention personnel.

Area/Regional managers will most likely have been employed for their retail skills and achievements, not investigation skills. Property/estates/facilities department staff will be required to know all about the security equipment, what it costs and where it can be purchased and HR/ personnel staff will need to learn all about manned guarding, including regulations and procedures.

Management

In order for this approach to work efficiently, it is recommended that at the very least there should be a loss prevention or risk management specialist employed to train, oversee, and advise individuals carrying out these joint responsibilities. This individual could also be used to conduct specialised or protracted investigations and for formulating the business loss prevention/ risk management policies and procedures.

Costs

In any line of business where a person 'wears more than one hat', that is to say they fulfil more than one role, financial savings will be made and this approach to loss prevention is no exception. Having acknowledged this fact any savings that could potentially be made by not financing dedicated 'in house' security specialists, could subsequently be lost as a result of the people assuming the roles not being as efficient. This is particularly so when it comes to addressing such issues as the reduction of unknown shrinkage and crime prevention etc.

Advantages

There is potentially only one advantage of operating non-dedicated security teams and that is the potential cost savings.

Disadvantages

The disadvantages of operating a non-dedicated security team are:

- There will always be a distinct lack of expertise in this area of the business
- Those responsible for the roles could potentially cost the business a lot of money by getting it wrong
- Important security matters may inadvertently take second place to the primary roles of those that have been delegated with the responsibility. This can especially be the case when they are under pressure to deliver in their primary roles.
- Dishonest staff may take advantage of the situation

Although it can be seen from the above analysis, operating non-dedicated security teams is a far from ideal situation but it is still better than no-one assuming these roles at all.

Third Party Security Specialists

Another approach to operating security functions within a business is third party security specialists. All of the roles described in the section above (security guards will be covered separately) can be fulfilled by hiring, on contract, security companies and freelance individuals that specialise in providing these services.

This method of providing specialist services for a business can be an especially advantageous approach for smaller businesses that would not benefit from, or could not afford, the funding of full time 'in house' security specialists.

Selection of third party personnel

When selecting third party security specialists it is important to establish what exactly their area of expertise is and whether it will be appropriate for the function that you wish them to undertake. Meetings should be held with the potential supplier where further discussions can place in order to:-

- Establish their suitability for the role(s) that they will be expected to fill
- View documentary evidence relating to their qualifications and experience
- Examine references supplied by existing and previous customers
- Examine their liability insurance
- Discuss their potential terms and conditions
- Prepare confidentiality clauses for the business
- Discuss the business's potential terms and conditions

- Discuss potential KPIs
- Establish their charge rates

Further checks should also be made with:

- Companies House, to confirm that the Company is legitimate
- Credit rating organisations to make sure that the business is not in financial trouble, which could potentially leave the contracting business with problems.
- Existing and previous customers in order to establish the veracity of the supplied references.

Costs

Even after shopping around third party suppliers of these kinds of services and negotiating deals for favourable hourly rates, if the selected Company is any good, it will still be more expensive per hour to hire their services than what it would to pay an employed person to do a similar job. However, the benefits of hiring third party security specialists are:

- that unlike someone permanently employed by the business, provided that the right contract has been negotiated, the specialist need only be employed to do specific security related tasks for short periods of time
- there are none of the added expenses mentioned above to consider.

An example of how this would work could be where it is believed that a member of staff is returning to the business premises during the early hours of the morning and stealing stock. A third party loss prevention investigator could be hired for a week to conduct observations of the premises, obtain photographic/CCTV evidence of the comings and goings, and then produce a narrative report and evidence package. This could then be used for internal disciplinary proceedings and by the police for a criminal prosecution.

This is also an efficient way of dealing with spates of shoplifting that can be pinpointed to specific times, such as school holidays. Third party store detectives could be hired specifically to cover retail outlets during these occasions, as opposed to a person being hired on a permanent basis, when most of the time there are no problems.

Advantages

The advantages of employing third party security specialists are:-

- They need only be hired for short periods of time
- They can be hired to deal with specific security issues
- They can be hired for short periods of time to cover staff shortfalls in permanent in house roles
- They can be paid on a results basis

- It can work out cheaper than employing permanent in house teams

Disadvantages

The disadvantages of employing third party security specialists are:-

If due to certain circumstances they are hired on a frequent as opposed to an infrequent basis, it can cost more in the long term to operate this way

Their working practices may not be compatible with those of the business

They may not function as well as an in house team could if they do not familiarise themselves with the business specific practises and procedures

Internal Security Guarding

Security guards are quite often directly employed by a business and are therefore classed as being in-house. The regulations concerning security guards operating within the security industry do not apply to in-house security guards, which means at the present time they do not have to be licensed. Having said that, it is always desirable if any security guards deployed on the company's premises are SIA licensed.

Personnel Selection

Security guards are quite often the first persons a member of the public comes into contact with or sees when visiting a business or a retail outlet. It is therefore essential that when selecting staff for these roles they will be able to create a good impression, both in their appearance and the way they communicate.

The fact that contract security guards, those that are not employed in-house, are now legally required to possess a valid SIA licence means that those that cannot obtain one, for whatever reason, try and secure positions where one is not required. It is therefore recommended that when selecting personnel for such positions it is stipulated in the job advertisement that they must be in possession of such a licence, even though it is not required. By doing this it will ultimately save time by automatically filtering out any potential non-desirables. Additionally, the fact that a security guard holds an SIA licence to operate means they have undergone four days of training and passed a criminal records check, both situations which are beneficial to any organisation wishing to employ them.

Once again, during the interview process consideration should be given to:-

- Previous experience in a similar role

- Documentary evidence of such experience
- Any additional training to that required for SIA Licensing
- Communications skills, both written and oral
- Their availability to work the proposed shift patterns
- Their references and reasons for leaving their last position
- Training

The training that applicants would have received in order to obtain their SIA licence would have been fairly comprehensive. Nonetheless they will still need to undergo additional, company specific training pertinent to the way the business operates and the role that they will be undertaking.

Security guards should also be encouraged to partake in additional, higher level training for the following reasons:

- It will motivate them and the role will not be seen as a dead end job
- It will encourage ambition, especially if as a result of the additional training they can achieve promotion and enhanced pay
- Ultimately the business will benefit from a better trained and well-motivated security guard
- It allows the company to promote from within

Costs

Operating in-house security guards can be an expensive way of providing such a service for the following reasons:

- High salaries will be required to attract the right calibre of security guard
- Business National Insurance Contributions
- Provision of Uniforms
- Additional costs for temporary cover for long term sickness
- Additional costs for temporary cover for maternity leave
- Training
- Payment of Company Bonuses
- Business contributions to pension schemes
- Incremental pay rises
- Potential overtime costs

Advantages

The advantages of operating with in-house security guards are:

- They usually perform to a higher standard than those supplied by third party companies
- They tend to be more effective at their jobs, especially if they are included in any company bonus schemes

- It is easier to address any problems directly with the security guard, than via the management chain of a third party supplier.
- Continuity of staff. It will always be the same staff on the same job each day

Disadvantages

The disadvantages of employing in-house security guards are:

- The costs, as previously detailed above
- Inflexibility of staffing levels, especially in the event of an extraordinary occurrence or event, such as a major incident or dealing with protestors

External Security guards

Where security guards are required and it is either not possible or impractical to operate an in-house set up, then the only alternative is to employ the services of an external or third party guarding company.

Company Selection

Having made the decision to employ a third party guarding company the following points should be considered before putting a contract out for tender:

- Are the guarding Company that are tendering approved contractors under the provisions of the Private Security

Industry Act (PSIA) 2001? A list of approved contractors is always available on the SIA website at http://www.sia.homeoffice.gov.uk/pages/acs-roac.aspx

- Are the companies able to supply security guards that are trained and experienced in the particular roles that they will be required to work in?

- Are the companies that are being invited to tender local or national companies? This could be of importance on occasions when replacement security guards are required at short notice

- The hourly charge rate and the rate the security guards will be paid. In cases where guarding companies charge their clients premium rates, but pay the security guards the absolute minimum, the motivation of the security guards can be seriously affected

- Do the tendering third party guarding companies have current and sufficient liability insurance?

- Will the tendering companies provide a dedicated accounts manager, so that there is an interface between the guarding Company and the business? This provision is essential in order to promptly resolve any issues concerning the services that the Company are supplying

- The duration of any proposed contract, together with the details of any 'get out' clauses relevant to either party
- Details of any expected incremental rises in hourly rates, for example on each anniversary of the contract
- Who will be responsible for ongoing training and to what standard?

Although the security guards will have undergone extensive training in order to obtain their SIA licence to operate, they will still need to undergo additional training pertinent to how the business operates and specific to the role that they will be undertaking.

A detailed set of Site Instructions (SI's) detailing exactly what the security guards will be expected to do will also need to be produced by the business and agreed by the guarding company. In the security industry these are known as assignment instructions and there should be a set, produced by the guarding company, for each location at which they have security guards deployed. The assignment instructions must be made easily available for the security guards to refer to at all times.

Costs

Using a third party guarding company is perhaps the cheaper option for providing security guards for a business. This is because an hourly rate is always negotiated with the guarding company that is usually all inclusive. This means that there are no additional costs that need to be taken into consideration such as the cost of uniforms, training and National Insurance contributions etc.

Advantages

The advantages of using a third party guarding company are:

- You can shop around the numerous guarding companies to find a company that will best meet the business requirements. There are some companies that provide security guards for specific Industries only and others that are able to accommodate more than one industry

- Because there are plenty of companies to choose from is possible to negotiate a good deal

- You can contract a guarding company for as many or as few hours as is necessary

- Greater flexibility. The number of security guards employed can by adjusted on a week by week basis if necessary.

- If a security guard should go sick, a replacement security guard is provided at the same hourly rate, and not at overtime rates

Disadvantages

The disadvantages of using a third party guarding company are:

- The standard of security guards that are supplied may not equate to the standard that would be employed by a business for an in-house set up

- The security guards supplied by third party guarding companies are not always as motivated as those employed by a business for an in-house set up

- Third party guarding companies can be unreliable

- It is sometimes difficult for third party guarding companies to supply the same security guards to the same sites all the time.

- Any issues with the security guards are normally addressed through their management chain, who are not based at the site. This can cause delays in resolving problems.

Do not make the mistake of contracting to the least expensive guarding company. The security industry works to very tight financial margins and companies will undercut each other just to survive. Ensure full background checks are conducted on any guarding company before contracting to them. Two of the UK's largest guarding companies have recently been investigated for serious fraud offences in respect of UK government contracts they had been awarded.

Conclusion

Physical security plays a large part in the loss prevention and profit protection effort in any retail business. Consideration has to be given to every aspect of the retail supply and sales chain when looking at physical security measures to protect the organisation's assets.

Other books in this series deal with other aspects of retail loss prevention. Some of the subjects discussed in this book are covered in greater detail in these other titles. The full list of books in the series is given below:

Introduction to Retail Loss Prevention

Physical Security in the Retail Environment

Protecting the Retail Outlet

Distribution Loss Prevention

Retail Investigations

Management of the Loss Prevention Function

Loss Prevention For Online-Retail and Retail Technology

About the authors

The Retail Loss Prevention series has been written by two retail loss prevention specialists who, combined, have over 60 years of experience in loss prevention and profit protection across many industries.

Tim Trafford BEM

Tim Trafford BEM has over 25 years of experience working in and managing loss prevention and investigation departments including hospitality, sports retail, supermarket chains and distribution. He currently holds a senior position in the loss prevention department of a well-known international distribution chain.

Ian Watts MCMI. MIPI. MSyI

Ian Watts has over 25 years of experience investigating losses in various industries and 15 years of experience in training managers and loss prevention personnel in several countries.

www.ingramcontent.com/pod-product-compliance
Lightning Source LLC
Chambersburg PA
CBHW051652170526
45167CB00001B/435